MY ANCESTORS CAME WITH THE CONQUEROR

Those who did, and some of those who probably did not

by

ANTHONY J. CAMP

1990

Published by

Society of Genealogists

14 Charterhouse Buildings
Goswell Road
London EC1M 7BA

First published 1988

Corrected reprint 1990

(c) Anthony J. Camp, 1988, 1990

ISBN 0 946789 02 9

INTRODUCTION

In 1931 a bronze tablet was set up in the Castle of Falaise in Normandy containing the names of 315 persons who are described as the Knights who fought at the Battle of Hastings on 14th October, 1066.

Unfortunately, English historians have accepted little of the evidence on which this list was based. Dr. T.R. Thomson examined the sources in an article in "The Genealogists' Magazine" in December, 1931 (vol. 5, pp. 394-7). That article, "The Falaise Celebrations", forms the first of the definitive group on the subject which are here reprinted. He concluded that the names of only fifteen 'Companions' could be accepted, of which twelve could be identified with tenants mentioned in Domesday Book.

Dr. Thomson's article aroused great interest and a discussion on the subject with W.T.J. Gun in the Chair, was organised at the Society of Genealogists on 13th February, 1932, at which Geoffrey H. White read an important paper confirming Dr. Thomson's conclusions. A report of that meeting was published in "The Genealogists' Magazine" (vol. 6, pp. 50-57) and forms our second article.

Here the matter rested until in 1944 Professor D.C. Douglas contributed a paper on "The Companions of the Conqueror" to "History" (vol. 28, pp. 129-147) in which he enumerated 27 Companions. Mr. White's extensive commentary on this article in "The Genealogists' Magazine" (vol. 9, pp. 417-424) forms the third of our articles. In it he accepted a total of nineteen Companions, of whom fifteen certainly and four almost certainly fought at Hastings.

Mr. White's conclusions have never been seriously challenged. From only one of those listed by him, William Mallet, can a probable descent in the male line to the present day be shown, though the early links have not been proven beyond doubt. Descents in the female line can be proved from several.

The above quoted historians had no hesitation in rejecting the so-called Battle Abbey Roll as a quite unreliable list of those present at the Battle. The genealogist John Horace Round had shown in "The Monthly Review" in 1901 (III, p. 97) that it was probably a fourteenth century production. The original was lost at some time in the eighteenth century. The Duchess of Cleveland, who lived at Battle Abbey, said in 1889 that there was a family tradition that the Roll had been taken from the Abbey by the Browne family to their other residence at Cowdray in 1717 and destroyed there in a fire in 1793. It survives only in several very unsatisfactory copies. Fuller said of a French copy [in his "Church History of England", 245-6], "I fear it hath passed through some butcher's hands

3

before it came to us. For there be three editions thereof in our English historians, which like the feet of a badger, fall out of unequal length, so different the number of names therein".

What appears to have been a 'copy' of the Roll was made by John Leland before 1550 and published by Thomas Hearne in 1715 [Number 5 in the appended Table]. Another 'copy' was printed in Raphael Holinshed's Chronicle in 1577 [Number 1 in the appended Table]. A third 'copy' made by Guillaume le Tailleur in 1487 was copied by Stowe and printed in 1615 [Number 6 in the appended Table] and again copied by Camden for Andre Duchesne who printed his version in 1619 [Number 3 in the appended Table]. In a well-known passage about the Roll Camden says, "Whosoever considers well shall find them always to be forged, and those names inserted which the time in every age favoured, and were never mentioned in that authenticated record".

There are other lists of persons who are said to have come over with the Conqueror but these do not pretend to have been taken from the Roll of Battle Abbey. The most important is perhaps that given in the Chronicle of John of Brompton, Abbot of Jervaulx in Yorkshire, compiled about 1436 and printed by Twysden in 1652 [Number 2 in the appended Table].

Several of these lists were published by Sir Bernard Burke in "The Roll of Battle Abbey, Annotated" (1848). With material from the historian Wace they formed the basis of J.R. Planche's "The Conqueror and His Companions" (2 vols. 1874) and the Duchess of Cleveland's "The Battle Abbey Roll" (3 vols. 1889).

Between 1925 and 1930 Walter Rye published an index to six versions of the Roll in "The Genealogists' Magazine", vols. 1-5, and it had been my intention to reprint that index here. I found, however, that it had been rather inaccurately compiled and I have gone back to the various lists and checked all the entries for the table which follows the introductory papers, adding two further lists. The eight versions there indexed include all those mentioned above, together with the names given by the historian Wace, discussed at length in the reprinted papers [Number 4 in the Table], and the list engraved on the monument at Falaise which started the argument in 1931 [Number 7 in the Table]. The names from an older list compiled by Leopold Delisle for the eighth centenary of the Battle in 1866 and engraved on a monument at Dives where William prayed before embarkation, and thus known as the Dives Roll, have also been included [Number 8 in the Table]. Further details of the contents of the table and of the abbreviations there used are given at its head.

Those persons accepted by Mr. White as having certainly or almost certainly been at the Battle of Hastings are shown in the table **in heavy type**.

4

(1)

THE FALAISE CELEBRATIONS

1931

[Reprinted from "The Genealogists' Magazine", vol. 5, pp. 394- 397.]

There is one aspect of last July's celebrations at Falaise which will claim the attention of genealogists. It has been stated in the Press that a bronze memorial has been set up in Falaise Castle to the honour of the Conqueror and his Companions in Arms. On this are shown the "names of the knights who fought at Hastings". Apparently under the inspiration of "M. Jackson Crispin, historien de New-York", a committee was set up to this end in May, 1929. So far, this committee has accepted 315 names of descendants of these Companions and of the Conqueror. In "L'Echo de Falaise" of the 17th June we are told that:

"The list of Companions inscribed on the tablet has been formed after two years of deep study of ancient documents, contemporary evidences of the Conquest, the texts of the earliest chroniclers, and the researches which have been made into this vexed question by historians of all countries throughout the centuries.

The committee, anxious only to inscribe the names of knights whose presence at the Battle of Hastings was absolutely established, has preferred to run the risk of making omissions (which may be filled up in the future) rather than to accept too generously all the demands which have been made. During the relatively short time which has been available for their researches, the committee has established this first list of 315 names. The committee looks forwarding to depositing in the Bibliotheque Nationale and in the Bibliotheque Municipale of Falaise, during next year, copies of a complete work in which will be given the reasons which have determined its choice.

As a foundation of its researches, the committee has first studied writers contemporary with the Conquest, namely, Guillaume de Poitiers, chaplain to Duke William; Guy, Bishop of Amiens, almoner to Queen Matilda, to whom is attributed a latin poem on the Battle of Hastings; Guillaume de Jumieges, whose 'Gesta Normanorum' was dedicated to the Conqueror; Roger du Mont and Robert Torigny, who continued this work; Orderic Vital, born 1075 in England, who in 1085 entered the monastery of Sainte-Evroult and spent several years in England securing evidence on the period of the Conquest; the poet Wace born in Jersey in 1100, author of 'Roman de Rou', in which he mentions 118 knights in the train of the Conqueror at Hastings. The tapestry of Queen Matilda, most truthful of documents contemporary with the battle, has been studied in like manner. Among the more recent works which have been of great help to the Committee, we may quote: Camden, Hearne, Thomas Fuller, Dugdale, Freeman, Augustin Thierry, Pluquet's edition of the 'Roman de Rou', annotated by Auguste Le Prevoste, the editions of Wace by Taylor and Malet; the amply documented work of Planche — "William the Conqueror and his Companions"; researches on Domesday Book, the researches of M. de Gerville, the "Norman People" [See J.H. Round in "The Ancestor", vol. II, 1902], the "Battle Abbey" of Cleveland, the extremely valuable works of Professor Prentout, of M. le Chanoine Poree, and numerous other works a list of which is too long to record here.

The lists of Companions which have already been published in past centuries have been studied with equal care. Among others are those of Battle Abbey by Leland, Hollingshed and Stow and similar copies by Duchesne; the list of Guillaume Tailleur in the "Chronicles of Normandy"; of William of Worcester, published by Hearne, of John of Brompton, of Fox, of Scriven, Matthew of Westminster, besides others more recent, and especially that of Dives edited by the eminent Leopold Delisle, member of the Institut, who unhappily has not given us a hint of the evidence upon which he based his identifications.

The work of the Committee is not yet finished. There are doubtless other Companions who fought at Hastings and whose names do not yet appear upon this memorial. Their presence once firmly established, these names will make a second memorial.

> "l'Association des Chevaliers de Hastings,
> pour le Comite:
> Jackson Crispin."

Apparently all the proofs of descent of the chosen 315 (19 of which are descendants of a Crispin) were submitted to the scrutiny of Professor Macary (Secretaire Generale de "Comite Guillaume le Conquerant", rue de Brebisson, Falaise). In the same journal of the same date is a good list of subscribers - apparently the 315. In each case the subscriber and his certified ancestor are given.

Two questions immediately present themselves:

(1) Can it be proved that any one man was a Companion to the Conqueror at the Battle of Hastings?

(2) If so, is it possible to prove the descent of a family of to-day from such a one?

Both questions of course depend on the exact interpretation of the word

6

"proof". In each case proof must devolve upon evidence, and in this case upon the evidence of dead men's writings.

Let us examine what evidence we have to establish the existence of a particular "Companion". Contemporary evidence is limited to:-

(a)   The Conqueror's biography by his chaplain William of Poitiers [The extant part of his "Gesta Guilielmi II ducis Normannorum" covers 1047-1086].

(b)   The Latin poem "Carmen de Bello Hastingensi" by Guy, Bishop of Amiens.

(c)   The Bayeux Tapestry [See "The Monthly Review", Dec. 1904].

About 13 individuals can be identified in these as being present at Hastings. In the next generation was the chronicler Orderic, whose evidence is almost equally sound when speaking of families connected with the Abbey of Saint-Evroul of which he was a monk [See Mr. H.A. Doubleday's letter to "The Times", 10th March, 1930]. There are also a few contemporary charters mentioning individuals who were of the expedition. From these latter we may add two names. Then come the departmental archives of Normandy, searched by J.H. Round when preparing for the Public Record Office the "Calendar of Documents Preserved in France", and found to contain no fresh relevant information.

The next near contemporary evidence that may be cited is Wace's "Roman de Rou", in which he gives 117 names, 73 of which are merely territorial and not individual. Modern scholarship has found him to be grossly inaccurate and quite unreliable. Andresen in his standard edition proved that Wace did not begin Part III before 1170 and puts the earliest possible date for his birth at 1110. Upon Wace only are based many of the modern works so carefully considered by the committee.

"The Roll of Battle Abbey" need not be considered. It was probably a fourteenth century production; it is, from internal evidence alone, absolutely unreliable, and there is no evidence to show that it was ever in the possession of the Abbey [See J.H. Round in "The Monthly Review", 1901, III, 97].

Looking down the list of authorities studied in "earnest research" one finds that for proof of "companionage" most of them are worthless.

In turning to the second question, which may or may not have occupied a larger share of the time of Professor Macary and his committee, we must again consider the evidence.

Supposing then that we have the names of 17 Companions at the battle, how can we prove their descent in blood to the present day? The blood of many a Companion is doubtless in most of us, but that is a matter of more concern to the sociologist than to the genealogist, who seeks a proven descent from a definite named person.

For the making of pedigrees from these happy warriors the next evidence occurs twenty years later in Domesday Book, where we have lists of tenants-inchief and tenants by knight's service. Can any of the above 17 be identified with persons therein mentioned? Here we can only be concerned with the balance of probability. Next after Domesday comes the great Roll of the Pipe for 1130, and its successors from 1156; and the next transcript of the feudal returns sent in by the tenants-in-chief in 1156. There remain a few cartularies of abbeys and priories, the majority of which are in manuscript. None of the above are intended to be genealogical writings (such as the Heralds Visitations), and the beginner can see at once the largeness of the desert and the long distances between the oases.

About eight of the Domesday tenants-in-chief and two tenants by knight's service are proven roots of foliage of to-day, and that is all. It is infinitely easier for anyone to prove a descent from the Conqueror himself, but with Royal Descents this article is not concerned.

The position is summarised thus:-

There are 15 proved or extremely probable "Companions".

Of these 12 can be identified with great probability with Domesday tenants, and we shall be very glad indeed to subject claims of descent from any of these to a thorough examination.

It will be appreciated therefore that the celebrations at Falaise, although admirable in their international effect, gastronomically laudable, and socially delightful, have no value whatsoever to serious genealogists. Genealogy is a "science" in its disregard of all emotional elements in the search for truth. To desire to be descended from one of those men who accompanied the Conqueror is comprehensible, but such a desire cannot absolve aspirants from the necessity of publishing some scientific and historical proof of their descent.

I have to thank Mr. G.H. White, F.R.Hist.S., for his valuable assistance.
T.R. Thomson.

2

THE COMPANIONS OF THE CONQUEROR AT THE BATTLE OF HASTINGS

Discussion Meeting, 13th February, 1932

[Reprinted from "The Genealogists' Magazine", vol. 6, pp. 50-57.]

At the request of the President, Lord Farrer, Mr. Gun took the Chair and outlined the general idea of the Discussion, which was suggested by the Celebrations at Falaise last summer. Several members of the Society had written requesting that the problems raised by the Celebrations should be considered by the Society, hence the article in the December number of the Magazine and the present Discussion.

Mr. Geoffrey H. White then read his paper. He said that he had no personal interest in the question, as he was not one of those fortunate persons descended from a gallant knight who would certainly have been at Hastings if the pedigree-makers had invented him in time. Indeed, he might claim to be one of the few persons in England not descended (so far as he knew) through the female line from William the Conqueror, although no doubt he might be deprived of that distinction any day by the researches of some too industrious genealogist.

No one could examine old pedigrees and peerage books without being convinced that an ancestor who came over with the Conqueror was formerly regarded as an appendage which no gentleman should be without, and that when a man rose in the world, one of his first cares was to adopt an eligible ancestor. And the adoption of an ancestor was in many ways a much easier operation than the adoption of a child. For instance, it would be difficult to adopt a child who did not actually exist, but there was no difficulty in adopting an imaginary ancestor. Again, a child usually had relatives already — even Bunthorne in "Patience", who never had a mother, confessed to an aunt — and their consent to the adoption had to be obtained; but a man who wished to adopt somebody else's ancestor never troubled about such formalities. Thus a really popular ancestor might accumulate quite a number of unconnected families as his descendants, much as a comet might develop a number of tails, or a Hollywood star collect a number of husbands; although he believed that the stars usually shed one husband before adopting the next. "Sic itur ad astra!".

One well-known instance of a popular ancestor was Hereward the Outlaw, known as the Wake since his first adoption, by the very ancient family of that name: one of the few surviving families with a genuine male descent from the twelfth century. Hereward really existed, unlike another very popular ancestor, that Sir Michael de Carrington who bore the banner of Richard Coeur-de-Lion in the Holy Land, although Richard himself died some centuries too soon to have heard of him.

As to the men who fought at Hastings, William certainly had some thousands under his command, but the names of less than twenty were recorded. The only authorities which could be regarded as trustworthy were the histories of William of Poitiers and of Orderic and the Bayeux tapestry. (The names had been written on a blackboard, and, turning to this, the speaker commented briefly on each in turn, beginning with the twelve enumerated by William of Poitiers). [The various details on each Companion I have transferred to the main alphabetical table following these articles. Editor.]

(1) Robert de Beaumont, afterwards Earl of Leicester
(2) Eustace, Count of Boulogne
(3) William of Evreux
(4) Geoffrey of Mortagne, afterwards Count of Perche
(5) William FitzOsbern, afterwards Earl of Hereford
(6) Aimery IV, Vicomte of Thouars
(7) Hugh de Montfort, Lord of Montfort-sur-Risle
(8) Walter Giffard, Lord of Longueville
(9) Ralf de Tosni, Lord of Conches
(10) Hugh de Grandmesnil
(11) William de Warenne, afterwards Earl of Surrey
(12) William Malet

Orderic copied the names given by William of Poitiers and added two others:-

(13) Turstin FitzRou
(14) Engenulf de Laigle

The only additional name yielded for the battle by the Bayeux Tapestry appeared to be that of Odo, Bishop of Bayeux, the Conqueror's stepbrother, afterwards Earl of Kent. He left an illegitimate son, from whom descended the great Norman house of Le Hommet, hereditary constables of Normandy. It would be easy to add the names of many who may have fought at Hastings, and of some who were most probably in the battle; but proof was wanting.

Some years ago Professor Prentout published a brochure on "Guillaume le Conquerant" (Caen, 1927), to which he added a "Liste Nouvelle des Compagnons de Guillaume qui combattirent a Hastings". This was based on two of the three authorities cited above, viz William of Poitiers and the Bayeux Tapestry - apparently he overlooked the fact that Orderic had given two names in addition to those copied from William — and on a much later authority, Wace. But as Wace did not write his account of the battle until more than a century after it was fought, the names given in his "Roman de Rou" cannot be relied on.

10

Thus he included Roger de Montgomery and Roger de Beaumont, and M. Prentout copied their names without question, although we know on the best authority, that both these great barons stayed behind in Normandy.

[Mr. Prentout adds the Bishops of Bayeux and Coutances to those named by William of Poitiers; and Odo's brother, Robert, Count of Mortain, and two vassals, Wadard and Vital, from the Bayeux Tapestry. As these are mentioned before the battle, there is no actual proof (apart from Odo), although a very strong presumption, that they took part in it. By a curious slip M. Prentout describes Geoffrey de Mortagne (No. 4 supra) as "Geoffroi fils de Rotrou, comte de Mortain", which is as different from Mortagne as Hereford from Hertford. Some of the names as given by M. Prentout from Wace may cause surprise. Surely Geoffrey "du Maine" should be "de Mayenne", although the form of the name in the "Roman" may be ambiguous, and it is most unlikely that Geoffrey de Mayenne joined the expedition. But who was Geoffrey of Maine? And why is the Ancestor of Hugh le Bigot, whose name Wace did not try to guess, given as Hugh? He was probably either the Robert who occurs in Normandy before the Conquest or the Roger who emerges in England shortly afterwards.]

Mr. White concluded with some remarks on the few remaining families which could trace a genuine male descent from a Domesday tenant of 1086, notably Fitzgerald, Carew, Gresley, and possibly St. John from tenants-in-chief, and Shirley and Wrottesley from subtenants.

Mr. Thomson said that it was not long ago that the "antiquary" kept abreast of all antiquarian knowledge. Now, no one person is even an all round genealogist. He specialises in a county, a type of record, a period, and so forth. Sooner or later all genealogists seek one another's advice. The speaker said that he had the advantage of treating this subject in the same way as the "average genealogist" — if there were such a creature. Lack of time and skill precluded more than an amplification of the article which he had been persuaded to write.

He desired to call attention to the fact that his article was concerned with "the names of the knights who fought at Hastings", the possibility of identifying such persons and of proving a descent therefrom.

He thought that it was the general feeling of the Society — the only general genealogical institution in this country which produced first class material, which is available for genealogists all the world over, without monetary profit to members, and with a simple desire to increase the sources of genealogical information — that the public should be protected against charlatans. He thought that he had their approval when he said that they felt a collective responsibility in the matter.

As to the knights of Hastings members will have seen a list of Professor Macary's elsewhere. What were the evidences of the existence of certain individuals at Hastings? In his opinion Wace was hopeless. Round had destroyed "The Norman People" (Anon., 1874) many years ago. The "Battle Abbey Roll" was a fourteenth century compilation. Planche, in so far as he relied on these, defeats himself. There are left: William of Poitiers, Guy, the Bayeux Tapestry, and Orderic.

The second difficulty — and this was where the challenge lay — was the proving of descent from these people. Mr. Thomson said that his article was not concerned with descents from Domesday tenants as such, or with descents from the Conqueror, but with the descents from the Companions at the Battle.

Many claims were based in some way on "surnames", and in conclusion Mr. Thomson showed how exceedingly easy it was to mistake identity, and that surnames, as the term was usually understood, began to crystallise among the upper classes towards the end of the twelfth century, and took over two hundred years to extend to the larger part of the population. The speaker then took an imaginary family and traced possible descents and nomenclature, illustrating his remarks by means of a chart.

The Chairman read Mr. Holman's paper. He proceeded to point out that Mr. White, Mr. Thomson and Mr. Holman were all agreed that the names of no more than 20 at most could be definitely established as having fought at Hastings and that there were now no descendants in the male line from any of these warriors. Besides the Conqueror himself, descents existed in the female line from perhaps ten of the known Companions. Anyone who could shew a descent from the medieval English baronage could probably show a descent from all of these. It was interesting to consider who were the heirs at line of these particular Companions. Prince Rupert of Bavaria is heir at line of the Conqueror, and among possible heirs at line of the others are the Baroness Kinloss, the Countess of Loudoun, Lord Mowbray and the Duke of Atholl, who between them largely represent the medieval baronage.

Mr. Townroe, Secretary of the United Associations of Great Britain and France, after thanking the Society for inviting some of those who went to Falaise to attend the Discussion, protested against some of the expressions, such as "charlatan", which had been used, holding these to be derogatory to distinguish French historians who had prepared the list of names of the 315 Companions of the Conqueror for the tablet at Falaise. Mr. Townroe read a letter from Professor Macary who stated that, owing to the unfriendly way in which the article in the "Genealogists' Magazine" was written, he was not prepared to enter into a discussion with the Society of Genealogists. Mr. Townroe then proceeded to refer to the coming festival at Hastings [8-11th July, 1932], to which he very kindly invited the members of the Society.

Colonel Clack, speaking both as a Fellow of the Society and as one who was present at Falaise, protested against the use of the word "ridiculous" in the Editorial of the December number of the Magazine, and against the insertion of frivolous verses on the subject of the Companions. He proceeded to say that in his opinion, Wace, who was largely relied upon by the French historians was as good an authority as those mentioned by Mr. White and Mr. Holman.

Mr. de Carteret put forward a plea for the probability that a de Carteret was a Companion of the Conqueror.

Dr. Moor remarked that he would like to know how the Falaise Committee obtained proof of the 315 names they had passed as Companions. Proof of each particular name would be most desirable. Unfortunately no record had been left of the names of those who embarked on the ships for Hastings. A muster-roll would have been invaluable.

Mr. Holworthy considered that help rather than ridicule should have been offered by the Society, but that proof must depend on the evidence available. On the whole his sympathies were with the proceedings of the Falaise Committee which had worthily commemorated a great historic event. In answer to a question Mr. Townroe stated that the 315 names placed on the tablet at Falaise were the names of those considered to be Companions and not, as some had supposed, the names of descendants of the Companions.

The Chairman observed that the French historians, in making the list of 315, do not appear to have consulted any English historians or genealogists. So far as this Society was concerned its attitude should be one of no acceptance without proof, more particularly in the matter of descents. There was no desire to give offence, but the whole position would be far more satisfactory if the extended list of the Companions and the descents claimed from them, could be subjected to a scientific analysis. In any case, however, the celebration would have done much good in ventilating the whole subject of Norman descents.

Mr. Thomson, in reply, referred to the objection to the use of the work "ridiculous", and to the demand for an apology. He did not consider that any apology was needed. All scientific persons whether biologists, astronomers, chemists, or historians, made known to the world the evidence upon which they based their new theories. Those who made assertions without publishing them, might rightly be called charlatans, and in any case to put up a lasting memorial first, and to publish evidence afterwards, seemed to the speaker ridiculous.

With regard to Wace. A witness in the box may tell a false-hood; it may be a slip. The same thing may occur two or three times, and the fasehoods may still be in the nature of "slips". If a large part of his evidence is false, he is, as a witness, discredited in toto.

13

The suggestion that a learned society should for political reasons refrain from voicing its opinion was laughable. The Society was only concerned with historical criticism, and in no way with the social or political aspect of the matter.

Lord Farrer, in conclusion, said that he had warned their friends who had so kindly attended, that genealogy, which ought to be the most peaceful of pursuits, was apt to develop passions more suited to the Field of Hastings itself than to the quiet rooms of Bloomsbury Square.

They were engaged, however, in a common endeavour to ascertain facts, and he was sure that they all knew their French friends were actuated by similar motives, for although a nominally Republican Nation, one of their favourite proverbs was "L'exactitude est la politesse des Princes".

Sir Walter Scott himself, Prince of Antiquarians, was also a man accustomed to evidence being exact, and laughed at himself through the mouth of Edie Ochiltree — "Pretorium here, pretorium there: I kenned the biggin o't".

They would go away to meet the very kind invitation to the field of Hastings in the summer (if there was to be a summer this year) and let them give their French friends every chance of solving the differences which he, the speaker, recollected fifty years ago as to the exact site of the battle between the rival historians of the day, Freeman and Stubbs, which was ended so happily (after even more heated language than had been heard that afternoon) by the Balliol poet's rhyme -

"And ladling butter from alternate tubs
Stubbs butters Freeman, Freeman butters Stubbs".

Lord Farrer then declared the Meeting closed.

3

COMPANIONS OF THE CONQUEROR
Lecture delivered to the Society of Genealogists on 10th May 1944
by Geoffrey H. White, F.S.A., F.R.Hist.S.

[Reprinted from "The Genealogists' Magazine", vol. 9, pp. 417- 424.]

No doubt some of those present will remember the very lively discussion which we held in the Society's old rooms in Bloomsbury Square, on the 13th February, 1932, when we tried to work out a list of those Companions of the Conqueror whose presence at the Battle of Hastings could be considered certain. On that occasion I was asked to open the discussion on behalf of the Society and submitted a list of 15 names of those whom I regarded as qualified. Two other representatives of the Society, Mr. Thomson and Mr. Holman, agreed in placing the total at under 20. Naturally this was not at all pleasing to those more credulous persons who had accepted as authentic the list of no less than 315 names, duly inscribed in 1931 on a tablet at Falaise.

There the matter rested until a few months ago, when Professor Douglas contributed a very able and interesting paper on "Companions of the Conqueror" to "History", the Journal of the Historical Association (Vol. XXVIII, pp. 129147). From this it was obvious that he was not aware of the discussion held by this Society 12 years ago and had approached the problem from an independent standpoint. It seemed to our Executive Committee that the Society should take some notice of the professor's paper and compare his results with our own; and I have had some very friendly correspondence on the subject with Prof. Douglas, whom I used to meet at the Royal Historical Society, before he went to the University of Leeds in 1939.

The Conquest may be said to cover the years 1066-70, although the fighting was not continuous. However, in our discussion we restricted our list to those who fought at the Battle of Hastings, and Prof. Douglas is concerned solely with the Hastings campaign. He ends his paper with a "Provisional List of those Persons whose Presence on the Expedition of 1066 appears to be established by express Evidence", in which he enumerates 27 Companions.

This limitation to the invasion of 1066 excludes, among others, two of the greatest barons in Normandy, Roger de Beaumont and Roger de Montgomery, both cousins of the Duke; for Roger de Beaumont was left in Normandy as chief adviser of the Duchess Maud [Note 1], and Roger de Montgomery was another of her counsellors, first coming to England with the Conqueror at the end of 1067 [Note 2]. Such later arrivals were not precluded from sharing in the spoils. Roger de Montgomery received the lordship of Arundel and Earldom of

Shrewsbury; and Roger de Beaumont had lands in Dorset and Gloucestershire [Note 3].

As explained above, while we confined our list to those present at the Battle of Hastings, Prof. Douglas has compiled a list of those who took part in the "Expedition of 1066". However, it is evident that by this he means only those men who actually landed in England; for he expressly excludes from his list a knight named Osmund de Bodes, on the ground that, although he started on the expedition, it seems doubtful whether he ever crossed the Channel [Note 4].

A charter of the Holy Trinity of Rouen relates that when William, Duke of the Normans, sought the land of the English, Osmund, having set out thither (illuc profectus) with others and having been attacked by illness and brought to extremities, made a gift to Holy Trinity for the salvation of his soul [Note 5]. I am not sure whether ad extrema perductus means that he actually died, or only thought that he was dying — an illusion said sometimes to be caused by the agonies of sea-sickness; but I think that the words illuc profectus prove that he had not been taken ill while the fleet was lying becalmed at the mouth of the Dives; so he either died at sea or reached England, although if he landed he may not have been fit to fight at Hastings [Note 6].

The Conqueror must have left a small force to guard his fortified base at Hastings, where he threw up a castle mound before proceeding inland, and there may have been a few casualties from accident or illness; but if a knight did land at Pevensey, it is almost certain that he fought at Hastings. On the other hand, a genealogist would not regard the fact as proof that he was in the battle.

Now at last we come to the Companions of the Conqueror. The AngloSaxon Chronicle does not mention the names of any men in the Duke's army, and William of Jumieges is equally devoid of information. The only contemporary historian who names any of them is William of Poitiers, who had lived in the Duke's household, and although he was not at the battle, is a firstclass authority. He names 12 men who fought in William's host, namely: Robert de Beaumont (son and heir of Roger de Beaumont), afterwards Count of Meulan and Earl of Leicester; Eustace, Count of Boulogne; William, afterwards 3rd Count of Evreux; Geoffrey of Mortagne, afterwards Count of Perche; William fitz Osbern, afterwards Earl of Hereford; Aimery, Vicomte of Thouars; Hugh de Montford, Lord of Montfort-sur-Risle; Walter Giffard, Lord of Longueville; Ralf de Tosni, Lord of Conches; Hugh de Grandmesnil, Lord of Grandmesnil; William de Warenne, afterwards Earl of Surrey; and William Malet, Lord of Graville [Note 7].

Besides these twelve, William of Poitiers mentions the two Bishops who were included in the expeditionary force [Note 8]. One of these was the Conqueror's half-brother, Odo [Note 9], Bishop of Bayeux, afterwards Earl of Kent; the other was Geoffrey de Mowbray, Bishop of Coutances. The historian says that the part of the bishops and monks was to pray; but if we turn to the Bayeux Tapestry, we find Bishop Odo, baton in hand, rallying the Normans who were fleeing before the English onslought; although whether he fought against the English army or only stopped the Normans in flight remains doubtful. The Bayeux Tapestry is the only other authority which stands on the same level as William of Poitiers; for although attempts have been made to show that it dates only from the XIIth Century, it is now generally recognized that the tapestry was begun soon after the battle and was probably finished before the death of the Conqueror. Unfortunately very few names are indicated; indeed, in the scenes depicting the battle the only other follower of the Duke whose name is shown is the Count of Boulogne, one of the twelve named by William of Poitiers. However, in the scenes between the landing and the battle three others are named. One is the Conqueror's younger half-brother, Robert, Count of Mortain, afterwards Earl of Cornwall. The others are Wadard and Vital, who are supposed to be identical with two tenants of the Bishop of Bayeux so named in Domesday Book, who were probably men of some local importance at Bayeuux. Adding these names to those mentioned by William of Poitiers, we have 17 Companions who took part in the Expedition of 1066; of whom 13 certainly, and the other 4 almost certainly, were present at the battle.

There is one other writer on whom we may rely, although he does not possess quite the same authority as William of Poitiers; for Orderic was not born until nearly ten years after the Battle of Hastings. However, he is generally trustworthy, and one of the proofs that he can be relied on in this connection, is that, when he wished to name the men who fought at Hastings, he went to the best authority and borrowed the list given by William of Poitiers. In his account of the battle he mentions two other men in the Norman Army. Turstin fitz Rou bore the Duke's banner. Nothing is known of his father, except the name, or of his antecedents; but it is practically certain that he was identical with the man of that name who subsequently held lands in the Welsh Marches. He seems to have died without issue. Engenulf de Laigle was killed late in the battle when the pursuing Norman cavalry fell into the "malefosse". Engenulf was son of Foubert de Beine, who built the castle of Laigle — so-called because the workmen found an eagle's nest in an oak near by — on the Risle. He was succeeded by his son, Richer de Laigle (slain in 1084), whose issue held the lordship of Pevensey, hence sometimes known as the Honor of the Eagle [Note 10]. Laigle, or the Eagle, was latinized as "de Aquila"; and Richer's younger brother was "Gilbert de Aquila" who will be known to the readers of Kipling's books, "Puck of Pook's Hill" and "Rewards and Fairies".

Adding these two names to the other 17, we have a total of 19 Companions, of whom 15 certainly and 4 almost certainly fought at Hastings. This completes the list of the Companions which we submitted as our tentative list a dozen years ago. These 19 names duly appear in the new list compiled by Prof. Douglas, and to these he has added 8 more names from various sources. Two of these are derived from different passages in Orderic's history; another two are taken from a Latin poem describing the Battle of Hastings, said to have been written by Guy, Bishop of Amiens; and the other four are derived from charters.

To begin with those from Orderic: he relates that Goubert d'Auffay took part in fights in the English War, but after the kingdom had been pacified and William had become King, he returned to Normandy, although the King offered him many possessions in England, because he was unwilling to possess any of the spoil [Note 11]. This may be regarded as proof that Goubert participated in the Expedition of 1066; nor can it be doubted that his fights would include the Battle of Hastings.

Again, after relating the doings of a certain Robert de Vitot in 1063, Orderic adds that not long afterwards, when the English War, in which he was wounded in the knee, had been accomplished, he contracted a mortal illness, from which he died [Note 12] (apparently at Dover). It is extremely likely that this refers to the Expedition of 1066 and that he was wounded at Hastings, although it is not impossible that the passage refers to later fighting.

The charters of the Holy Trinity at Rouen yield three names for Prof. Douglas's list. Roger, son of Turold, when about to voyage overseas with Count William, made a gift to this Abbey; but because he could not confirm it, being prevented by death in the same voyage (navigatione), a certain knight of his did so [Note 13]. This is clear proof that Roger started on the Expedition of 1066; but we are left in doubt as to whether he died before or after the Battle of Hastings or was killed in the Battle. Strictly navigatione would imply that he died at sea, but it would be rash to insist on this literal translation.

In another charter a certain Oger de Panilleuse gave a vineyard to Holy Trinity, partly for the salvation of the soul of his brother Gerelm, lately deceased in England [Note 14]. Prof. Douglas assumes that Gerelm fought and died in the Hastings campaign, which is very likely; but as the charter cannot be dated exactly, it is possible that he was killed in one of the later campaigns, or died during a peaceful interval.

Another charter, which Prof. Douglas is able to date within the limits Feb. to Dec. 1067, records that the monks have redeemed a moiety of the chapel of Holy Trinity by giving six pounds to Erchembald, son of Erchembald the Vicomte, setting out overseas, and twelve pounds to Hugh de Ivry the Butler, who held it on Mortgage from the said Erchambald; William, King of the English and Duke of the Normans, and his nobles assenting [Note 15]. Prof. Douglas thinks that there can be no doubt that Erchambald's journey overseas had taken place in the Duke's army in the previous year. To me it seems more likely that the transaction took place when the Conqueror was about to revisit England in Dec.

18

1067 and that the charter refers to Erchembald's coming voyage in his company. Of course this would not imply that Erchembald had not taken part in the Expedition of the previous year. Indeed, it would seem not unlikely that he had mortgaged his property to Hugh de Ivry in 1066, in order to raise funds for that expedition; and possible that both men sold their rights to Holy Trinity in 1067 in order to obtain money for the expedition of that year. However, that is only a conjecture.

Another man whom Prof. Douglas supposes to have fought at Hastings, and to have been killed there, is Robert fitz Erneis. This belief is based on a charter of the Abbey of Fontenay, issued by a descendant of Robert in 1217, which purports to recite earlier charters granted by his ancestors. However, the text of these is very confused, a charter of Robert fitz Erneis, who was living at the time of the Conquest, being mixed up with a charter of his son, Robert fitz Robert. The latter states that his father, Robert fitz Erneis, was killed in England in the time of the Conqueror, and makes it clear that this happened before the death of Queen Maud; i.e. within the years 1066-1083 [Note 16]. Prof. Douglas writes that this "establishes the truth of the assertion by Wace that Robert fitz Erneis fought and died at Hastings". I suggest that it is equally possible that Robert died in England on some other occasion, but that by the time when Wace wrote his account of the battle, more than a century later, a tradition had grown up that Robert was killed in the famous battle; or again that Wace was told that Robert had died in England and thought that it would provide an interesting incident for his poem to kill him off in the battle. All this is on the assumption that these charters are authentic; but they are not above suspicion. Robert fitz Robert is made to give the name of his mother, the wife of Robert fitz Erneis, as Hawise; but according to a record of 1106, which seems to be genuine, her name was Gersende [Note 17]. Again, a charter of Robert, Count of the Normans, dated 1091, bears the "Signum Rotberti Herneis" [Note 18], which looks like the Robert fitz Erneis alleged to have been killed not later than 1083.

The last two Companions in the Professor's list are taken from a Latin poem on the Battle of Hastings [Note 19], attributed to Guy, Bishop of Amiens from 1058 to 1076. It is certain that Guy did write such a poem, which is mentioned by Orderic and Robert de Torigny [Note 20]. Although there is no proof that the extant poem, which survives in a 12th century MS. at Brussels, is the bishop's work, it answers to the description given by Orderic [Note 21], and prima facie it seems unlikely that another such poem would be written so soon afterwards. That it is the bishop's poem is generally assumed by historians, including Prof. Douglas, who points out that it is from this poem that: "in the first instance is derived the account of the opening of the battle by the exploits of a minstrel (histrio) nicknamed 'Incisor Ferri', who went before the Norman host and continued singing and juggling with his sword until he was slain". Again, this poem relates how near the end of the battle the body of the dying Harold was mutilated by four men, three of whom — Eustace, Count of Boulogne, Hugh de

Montfort and Walter Giffard — are included in the twelve named by William of Poitiers. The fourth is not named, being mentioned vaguely as the noble heir of Ponthieu. Now both these truly remarkable incidents are ignored by our three highest authorities: William of Poitiers, the Bayeux tapestry and Orderic, as well as by William of Malmesbury, who comes next to them in date and trustworthiness. Yet if these things had really happened, they must have been matters of public notoriety; and if the existing poem is the work of Bishop Guy, our earliest authorities were acquainted with it. Why do they all ignore these two outstanding incidents of the battle? For the same reason, I have no doubt, that they ignored the poet's statement that the Duke slew two thousand English himself, besides the other countless thousands killed (lines 555-6). They knew that all these exploits were fictions, invented by a poet to embellish his poem. The mountebank Taillefer [Note 22] seems a figure of romance rather than of history.

As to the alleged killing and mutilation of the dying Harold, the story is not only ignored by all the best authorities, but is unlikely in itself and incompatible with such accounts as we have of his death; as indeed was pointed out long ago by J.R. Planche, who also argued that the Count of Boulogne had been disabled at an earlier stage of the battle [Note 23]. Even the later poet Wace, who adopted the Taillefer story, drew the line here and admitted that he had never heard who killed the King [Note 24].

Moreover, who was the noble heir of Ponthieu? Bishop Guy knew, for he was uncle of the reigning Count, Guy I, the man who had seized Harold when he was driven ashore on the coast of Ponthieu. Guy had a son, Enguerrand, whose existence is known only from a charter of his parents, making a gift of salt to St. Martin des Champs, for the salvation of their souls and the soul of their son Enguerrand. Unfortunately this charter may have been granted at any time within 1053-90, and the absence of any other mention of the boy suggests that he died young. He certainly died v.p., for Guy, in a charter granted 6 Oct. 1100, acknowledged that the heir to Ponthieu was Earl Robert de Belleme, by reason of Robert's marriage to his first-born daughter Agnes [Note 25]. Agnes had married Robert before the death of the Conqueror [Note 26]; but girls married young in those days, and it is very doubtful if she were born so early as 1066. The possibility of her brother, even if he were born by 1066, being old enough to fight at Hastings seems negligible. If Enguerrand and his two sisters were not yet born in 1066, the heir was Count Guy's uncle, Bishop Guy the poet, who was not at Hastings [Note 27]. No other member of the family seems to be known, and if one did exist, he would not be the heir. Prof. Douglas suggests that the poet may mean the Count himself, which is not impossible; but it is difficult to understand why the poet, after naming the other three men, should refer to his nephew in such a roundabout way, or why, if he fought at Hastings, he did not share in the spoils [Note 28]. In fact, I agree with Planche in rejecting the whole story, and go beyond him, by disbelieving the Taillefer story as well.

The question whether the poem should be treated as sober history or as romance is really a matter of opinion, and I fear that historians will hold that genealogists have unduly suspicious minds.

In conclusion, although I have ventured to differ from Prof. Douglas on some questions, and to suggest doubts on others, I am sure that all genealogists will be grateful to him for the new light which he has shed on the subject. It is all to the good that it has at last been tackled seriously by an historian, and especially by an historian of the standing of Prof. Douglas, who is one of our leading authorities on the period [Note 29].

Notes

(1) Will. Poitiers, in Duchesne, Hist. Norm. Scriptores, p. 211.

(2) Ord. Vit. (ed. Le Prevost), vol. ii, p. 178. It is quite likely that Robert de Torigny was correct in stating that Roger "bello Anglico interfuit" (William de Jumieges, ed. Marx, p. 322, interpolations), though too late for the earlier campaigns.

(3) Domesday Book, vol. i, pp. 80, 168. Round stated that part, and possibly the whole, of the Warwickshire fief held by his son Robert in 1086 had first been held by Roger (Cal. Docs. France, pp. xlix-l); but the charter on which he relies (No. 318) is suspicious, Roger's younger son Henry being styled Earl of Warwick before he was created an earl.

(4) History, vol xxviii, p. 142, note 7.

(5) Chart. Mon. S. Trin., ed. Deville, No. LVII (p. 451).

(6) The word used for illness is not aegritudo, as in Charter No. LV, but langor (languor); which is the word used by the Melrose Chronicle in connexion with the death at sea of the 3rd Earl of Leicester in 1191. See Genealogists' Magazine, Vol. 9, p.350.

(7) Will. Poitiers, op. cit., pp. 202, 204. For some details of the twelve see The Genealogists' Magazine, Vol. 6, pp. 51-53, and Prof. Douglas's paper.

(8) Will. Poitiers, op. cit., p. 201.

(9) Odo was the Latinized form of his name; but he is so well known as Odo that it might seem pedantic to call him Eudes.

(10) Ord. Vit., vol. ii, pp. 147, 150, 295; vol. iii, p. 197. Richer's son Gilbert appears in Domesday Book.

(11) Ord. Vit., vol. iii, p. 44. Prof. Douglas points out that Orderic obtained his information from Goubert's son Hugh, who became his fellow-monk at St. Evroul.

(12) Bello Anglico, ubi et ipse in genu vulneratus est, peracto, lethiferam aegritudinem incurrit (Ord. Vit., vol. ii, p. 105). This does not seem to imply that the illness resulted from the wound, as Prof. Douglas assumes.

(13) Chart. S.T. Rouen, No. LXIII (pp. 453-4).

(14) Ibid., No. XV (p. 430). Prof. Douglas treats this as the confirmation of gifts by Gerelm, but the record does not say so.

(15) Ibid., No. XLVII (p. 446).

(16) Gallia Christiana, Vol. xi, Instr., col. 333-4.

(17) Round, Cal. Docs. France. No. 425.

(18) Chart. S.T. Rouen, No. LXXXIII (pp. 463-4).

(19) Printed by Petrie, Monumenta Historica Britannica, and Giles, Scriptores Rerum Gestarum Willelmi Conquestoris.

(20) Ord. Vit., Vol. ii, pp. 158, 181; Will. de Jumieges (ed. Marx), p. 264 (additions by R. de Torigny). According to Orderic, he had written the poem before he came to England in 1068.

(21) Hardy, Materials relating to the History of Great Britain and Ireland (Rolls Ser.), Vol. i, pp. 671-2 (No. 1269). Hardy suggests an objection to identifying this poem with that written by Guy, but seems inclined to accept the ascription. His hesitation is duly noted by Planche, Conqueror and his Companions, Vol. i, pp. 170-1.

(22) That poet calls him "histrio" — an actor; later "mimus" (lines 391, 399), a word which occurs elsewhere in the sense of a player on musical instruments (Ducange, in voce). Henry of Huntingdon, the earliest historian to swallow the story, calls him cautiously "Quidam ... nomine Taillefer" — a certain man named Taillefer, and makes him juggle with swords (Rolls Series, pp. 202, 203). The performance did not include swallowing them. The poet Gaimar calls him a "Ioglere" and "iugleor" (Lestorie des Engles, Rolls Series, Vol. i, p. 223), i.e. a minstrel; which may be an attempt to make the affair more credible.

(23) Planche, op. cit., Vol. i, pp. 157-60, 171-2.

(24) Wace, Roman de Rou (ed. Andresen), Vol. ii, p. 382.

(25) Brunel, Recueil des Actes des Comtes de Ponthieu, Nos. vi, viii. Robert de Belleme was Earl of Shrewsbury, being son of Roger de Montgomery by Mabel de Belleme. For Mabel's ancestors see my paper on "The First House of Belleme", in Transactions R. Hist. Soc., 4th Ser., Vol. xxii, pp. 67-99.

(26) Ord. Vit., vol. iii, p. 300. Robert was born 10 years before the Conquest, perhaps rather earlier.

(27) He came to England in 1068 with Queen Maud (Ord. Vit., Vol. ii, p. 181).

(28) If the poem is not Bishop Guy's, the author may not have known who the heir of Ponthieu was in 1066, and the date would probaly be later than William of Poitiers and the Bayeux Tapestry.

(29) Prof. Douglas's article on "The Ancestors of William fitz Osbern", in the English Historical Review for Jan. 1944, is the most important contribution made to Norman genealogy for many years, and must be mentioned here, because William was one of the 12 Companions.

THE BATTLE ABBEY ROLL

The following list brings together references to the various versions of the so-called Battle Abbey Roll with details from the contemporary historians and other sources of varying reliability as discussed in the introductory papers printed above. Each surname is followed by a series of numbers from one to eight. These are references to the various versions of the Battle Abbey Roll and to the Falaise and Dives Rolls as listed below. In brackets after the number is the name as it appears on that Roll. Practically no christian names appear on any versions of the Battle Abbey Roll.

Then follow such references to that name as appear in Domesday Book in 1086. The Tenants in Chief are distinguished from the Sub-Tenants by the letters TC and ST after the date of the survey. These references, which are not exhaustive, are taken from the lists in "A General Introduction to Domesday Book; Accompanied by Indexes ..." by Sir Henry Ellis (2 vols., 1833).

Then follow references to 'Cleveland' and 'Loyd' giving details of the pages on which further information may be found in "The Battle Abbey Roll: with some Account of the Norman Lineages" by the Duchess of Cleveland (3 vols., 1889) and "The Origins of some Anglo-Norman Families" by Lewis C. Loyd (Harleian Society, vol. 103, 1951). The Duchess mixes fact with much fiction and I have some hesitation in including references to her work next to those of the scholarly Loyd. Where the Duchess of Cleveland has assumed in the Roll some corruption of a later known name her identification is given in brackets after the volume and page number, e.g. ANUAY, Cleveland I 24-26, 342 (=d'Aufay).

The eight lists of people said to have been at the Battle are taken from the following authorities:
1. The Battle Abbey Roll as published by Raphael Holinshed in his "Chronicles of England, Scotlande, and Irelande" (1577). These names are printed in Cleveland, I, xix-xxvii, and in "Falaise Roll", pp. 207-213.

2. The Battle Abbey Roll as given in the Chronicle ascribed to John Brompton, about 1436, and printed in Twysden, "Historiae Anglicanae Scriptores" (1652). These names are printed in "Falaise Roll", pp. 201-202.

3. The Battle Abbey Roll as published by Andre Duchesne in his "Historiae Normannorum" (1619). These names are printed in parallel with Holinshed's Roll, with which there are many similarities, in Cleveland, I, xix-xxvii, and in "Falaise Roll", pp. 207-213.

4. The Battle Abbey Roll as given by Robert Wace and published in "Master Wace, his Chronicle of the Norman Conquest from the Roman de Rou" by

Edgar Taylor in 1837. The names are printed in "Falaise Roll", pp. 200-201.

5. The Battle Abbey Roll as copied before 1550 by John Leland in his "De Rebus Britannicis Collectanea" and printed by Thomas Hearne in 1715. These names are printed in Cleveland, I, xxviii-xxx, and in "Falaise Roll", pp. 205-207.

6. The Battle Abbey Roll as given by Guillaume le Tailleur in his "Chronieques de Normendie" in 1487 and printed in "Annales or Generall Chronicle of England", begun by John Stowe and published by Edmond Howes in 1615. These names are printed in "Falaise Roll", pp. 203-205.

7. The Falaise Roll; the names of "Les Compagnons de Guillaume 1er Duc de Normandie a Hastings MLXVI" as given on the bronze tablet erected in the Chapel of the Chateau of William the Conqueror at Falaise, Normandy, 21 June 1931, and illustrated in "Falaise Roll", p. ix. Further details of these persons, again inextricably mixing fact with fiction, are to be found in "Falaise Roll: recording Prominent Companions of William, Duke of Normandy, at the Conquest of England" by M. Jackson Crispin and Leonce Macary (London, 1938; reprinted, with an important critical note by G. Andrews Moriarty, Baltimore, 1969 & 1985).

8. The Dives Roll of Leopold Delisle; a list of "Companions of William the Conqueror at the Conquest of England in 1066" compiled by Leopold Delisle for the eighth centenary of the Battle in 1866 and inscribed on a marble memorial erected in the church at Dives, where William prayed before embarkation. It was published by de Magny in his "Nobiliare de Normandie" [with a few additional names not indexed here] and was probably first published in England as an Appendix to the second edition of Sir Bernard Burke's "Vicissitudes of Families", 3rd Series, 1863. It was reprinted in Cleveland, I, xxxi-xxxv, and in "Falaise Roll", pp. 216-219. In many instances the list seems to be taken from Domesday Book, but as the Duchess of Cleveland said "it is to be regretted that he has in no case cited an authority or given a reference".

Those persons accepted by Mr. G.H. White in the introductory papers as having certainly or almost certainly been at the Battle of Hastings are distinguished **in heavy type.**

ABBETOT see ABETOT
ABBEUILE see ABBEVILE
ABBEVILLE
1 (Abbeuille)
4 (Wiestace d'Abevile)
Cleveland I 26-30
ABEL
1 (Abell)
3 (Abel)
Cleveland I 18-19
ABELL see ABEL
ABERNON
1 & 3 (Dabernoune)
5 (Dabernoun)
7 (Roger d'Abernon)
8 (Roger d'Abernon)
Rogerius de Abernon 1086 ST
Cleveland I 320-321
Loyd I
ABETOT
1 (Dabitot)
7 (Ours d'Abbetot)
8 (Ours d'Abbetot)
Vrso de Abetot 1086 TC
Cleveland I 349-350
Loyd 1-2
ABEVILE see ABBEVILLE
ABITOT see ABETOT
ABRINCIS see AVRANCHES
ACHARD
8 (Achard)
ACHIGNEIO see AKENY
ACQUIGNY see AKENY
ADGILLAM
1 (Adgillam)
2 (Aguloun)
3 (Angilliam)
Cleveland I 9-11
(=Angeloun)
ADOUBE
8 (Ruaud l'Adoube)
ADRECI see ARCY
ADRYELLE
5 (Adryelle; twice)
Cleveland III 355
AGANTEZ
2 (Agantez)
AGULIS
2 (Agulis)
AGULOUN see ADGILLAM
AIGLE, L', see LAIGLE
AIGNEAUX
7 (Herbert d'Aigneaux)
AIMERIS
5 (Aimeris)
Cleveland III 355-356

AINCOURT
1 (Aincourt) Irl
5 (Deyncourt)
7 (Gautier d'Aincourt)
Walterius de Aincurt 1086 TC
Cleveland I 6-9
Loyd 2
AIOUL
8 (Aioul)
AKENY
1 & 3 & 5 (Akeny; Dakeny)
Cleveland I 37-38
Loyd 2
ALBEMARLE see AUMALE
ALBENY see AUBIGNY
ALBINGI see AUBINGY
ALBINI see AUBIGNY
ALDRIE
Loyd 3
ALENCON
8 (Bernard d'Alencon)
ALFAIT see AUFFAY
ALIS
7 (Guillaume Alis)
8 (Guillaume Alis)
Willelmus Alis/Alisius
1086 TC
ALNEI
4 (Cil d'Alnei)
7 (Fouque d'Aulnay)
ALNOU
4 (Sire d'Alnou)
7 (Fouque d'Aunou)
8 (Raoul d'Aunou)
ALRE
7 (Guillaume d'Alre)
ALSELIN
8 (Geoffroi Alselin)
Goisfridus Alselin
(et Radulphus
nepos ejus) 1086 TC
ALTIFAGIUM see AUFFAY
ALUERS
Robertus de Aluers 1086 TC
AMAY
1 (Amay)
5 (Damay)
Cleveland I 43
AMBLIE
Loyd 3
AMBRIERES
7 (Achard d'Ambrieres)
AMERINGES see AVRANCHES
AMFREVILLE see UMFRANVILLE
AMIOT see DAMNOT
AMONDEVILLE see AMUNDEVILLE

AMONERDUILE see AMUNDEVILLE
AMORY
  1 & 3 (Damry)
  5 (Damary)
  Willelmus de Dalmari 1086 TC
  Cleveland I 321-323
AMOUERDUILE see AMUNDEVILLE
AMUNDEVILLE
  1 (Amouerduile)
  3 (Amonerduile)
  7 (Roger d'Amondeville)
  Cleveland I 31-33
  Loyd 3-4
ANDELI
  8 (Richer d'Andeli)
  Richerius de Andeli 1086 TC
ANDEUILE
  1 (Andeuile)
  2 (d'Andevile)
  4 (Cil de Val de Saire)
  Cleveland I 30-31
ANE see LANE
ANESIA see ANISY
ANGENOUN
  1 & 3 (Angenoun)
  Cleveland I 21-22
ANGENS
  Loyd 4
ANGERS
  1 (Angers)
  2 (d'Angiers)
  3 (Avvgers)
  Cleveland I 20-21
ANGERVILLE
  7 (Auvrecher d'Angerville)
  8 (D'Auvrecher d'Angerville)
ANGIERS see ANGERS
ANGILLIAM see ADGILLAM
ANISIE see ANISY
ANISY
  4 (Li jovente d'Anisie)
  7 (Le Sire d'Anisy)
  Loyd 4-5
ANNEVILLE
  7 (Guillaume d'Anneville)
ANSGOT
  8 (Ansgot)
ANSLEVILLE
  8 (Guillaume d'Ansleville;
    Honfroi d'Ansleville)
ANUAY
  1 (Anuay; Danway)
  2 (Danvey)
  3 (Danway)
  Cleveland I 24-26, 342 (=d'Aufay)
  see also AUFFAY

ANVER
  2 (d'Anver)
APPEVILLE
  7 (Gautier d'Appeville)
  8 (Fouque d'Appeville)
  Loyd 4-5
AQUILA see LAIGLE
ARCHER
  1 (Archere)
  3 (Archer)
  7 (Guillaume L'Archer)
  8 (Guillaume L'Archer)
  Cleveland I 22-24
ARCY
  1 & 2 (Arcy)
  5 (Darcy)
  8 (Norman d'Adreci)
  Norman de Adreci 1086 TC
  Cleveland I 33-37
ARDRE
  7 (Arnoul d'Ardre)
  8 (Arnoul d'Ardre)
AREY
  3 (Arey)
ARGENTAN see ARGENTEYN
ARGENTEN see ARGENTEYN
ARGENTEYN
  1 (Argentoune)
  2 (Argenten)
  3 (Argentoun)
  5 (Argenteyn)
  8 (David d'Argentan)
  David de Argentomago
    /Argentomo 1086 TC
  Cleveland I 11-13
ARGENTOUN see ARGENTEYN
ARGOUGES see ARGUGES
ARGUGES
  7 (Le Sire d'Argouges)
  8 (D'Argouges)
  Loyd 5
ARMENTIERES
  8 (Robert d'Armentieres)
ARQUES
  6 (Guilliam de Hoimes;
    Darques)
  7 & 8 (Guillaume d'Arques;
    Osberne d'Arques)
  Osbernus de Arches 1086 TC
  Osbertus de Archis 1086 TC
  Willelmus de Arcis 1086 TC
  Loyd 5-6
ARRAS
  2 (Arras)
ARTOYS
  2 (Artoys)

27

ARUNDELL
1 & 3 (Arundell)
7 & 8 (Roger Arundel)
Rogerius Arundel 1086 TC
Cleveland I 13-16
ASCELIN
7 (Geoffroi Ascelin)
ASINUS see LANE
GASNE see LANE
ASNIERES
4 (Gilbert d'Asnieres)
7 (Gilbert d'Asnieres)
ASPEREMOUND
1 (Aspermound)
3 (Asperemound)
Cleveland I 43-33
ASPERMOUND see ASPEREMOUND
ASPERUILE
1 & 3 (Asperuile)
Cleveland I 26
AUBEMARE
4 (Sire d'Aubemare)
AUBENAY see AUBIGNY
AUBERVILLE
2 (Aubevyle)
8 (Robert d'Auberville;
Roger d'Auberville;
Seri d'Auberville)
Rogerus (de) Oburuilla/
Otburuilla/Otburvilla
1086 TC & ST
Seric de Odburcuilla 1086 ST
Willelmus de Odburvile
seu Odburguille 1086 TC
Rotbertus/Robertus de
Odburvile/Otburguile
1086 TC & ST
Cleveland I 42-43
AUBIGNY
1 (Albeny; Daubeny)
3 (Albeny)
4 (Li boteillier d'Aubignie)
5 (Daubenay)
6 (Le Boutellier Daubegny)
7 (Le Sire d'Aubigny)
8 (Neel d'Aubigny)
Nigellus de Albingi 1086 TC
Cleveland I 38-42, 290-291
Loyd 7
AUCHENVILLA see AUKENVILLA
AUDEL
5 (Audel)
AUDELEY
1 & 3 (Audeley)
Richer de Andeli 1086 TC
Cleveland I 9

AUDRIEU
7 & 8 (Guillaume d'Audrieu)
AUENANT
1 & 3 (Auenant)
Cleveland I 16-18
AUFFAY
7 (Guilbert d'Aufay)
8 (Goubert d'Aufay)
Loyd 8 (see also ANUAY)
Orderic relates that Goubert d'Auffay took part in
fights in the English War, but after the kingdom had
been pacified and William had become King, he
returned to Normandy, although the King offered
him many possessions in England, because he was
unwilling to possess any of the spoil [Orderic
obtained his information from Goubert's son Hugh,
who became his fellow-monk at St. Evroul]. This
may be regarded as proof that Goubert participated
in the Expedition of 1066; and it cannot be doubted
that his fights would include the Battle of Hastings.
AUGUM see EU
AUKENVILL
Loyd 8
AULNAY see ALNEI
AUMALE
1 (Aumarle)
3 (Aumerle)
5 (Aumarill)
8 (Robert d'Aumale)
Robertus de Albemarle
1086 TC
Cleveland I 6
Loyd 9
AUMARILL see AUMALE
AUMARLE see AUMALE
AUMERLE see AUMALE
AUNE
8 (Guillaume de l'Aune)
AUNGELOUN
5 (Aungeloun)
AUNEWYNE see ANGENOUN
AUNOU see ALNOU
AUNWERS
1 (Aunwers)
AURIS
2 (Auris)
AUUERNE
1 (Auuerne)
Cleveland 1 19-20
AUVILER see AVILERS
AVENEL
2 (Avynel)
5 (Avenel; Avenele)
Cleveland III 353-355
AVENERIS
5 (Aveneris)

AVILERS
    4 (Sire d'Auviler)
    7 (Le Sire d'Auvillers)
    Loyd 9
AVRANCHES
    1 (Amerenges; Dauonge)
    5 (Daverenges)
    7 (Richard, Vicomte
        d'Avranches)
    8 (Hugue d'Avranches)
    Cleveland I 44-47, 328
    Loyd 9-10
AVRE
    8 (Rahier d'Avre)
AVRENCIN
    4 (Richarz d'Avrencin)
AVVGERS see ANGERS
AVYNEL see AVENEL
AYBEUARE
    1 (Aybeuare)
    Cleveland I 42-43
    (=Aubevale)
AZOR
    8 (Azor)
BACHEPUIS
    Loyd 10
BACHEPUZ see BACHEPUIS
BACON
    7 (Guillaume Bacon,
        Sire du Molay)
    Loyd 10-11
BACUN see BACON
BACY
    6 (Le sire de Bacy)
BADVENT see BAVENT
BAGOT
    1 (Bagot)
    Cleveland I 194-195
BAGPUZ see BACHEPUIS
BAIGNARD see BAINARD
BAILIF
    1 (Bailif)
    3 (Baylife)
    5 (Baillof)
    Cleveland I 76-81 (=Baliol)
BAILIOLIO see BAILLEUL
BAILLEUL
    6 (Pierre de Baillieul)
    7 (Le Sire de Bailleul)
    8 (Renaud de Bailleul)
    Rainaldus de Balgiole/
        Bailgiole 1086 TC
    Cleveland I 76-81
    Loyd 11-12
BAILLOF see BAILIF
BAINARD

    1 (Bainard)
    8 (Raoul Baignard;
        Geoffroi Bainard)
    Radulfus Baignard/Bangiard
        /Baniardus 1086 TC
    Gaosfridus Bainard 1086 ST
    Willielmus Bainardus 1086 ST
    Cleveland I 163-165
BAION see BAYEUX
BAIOUS see BAYEUX
BAIUS see BAYEUX
BALADONE see BALLON
BALGIOLE see BAILLEUL
BALLIEUL see BAILLEUL
BALLON
    1 (Baloun)
    2 (Baylon; Bayloun)
    5 (Bealum)
    7 & 8 (Guineboud de Balon;
        Hamelin de Balon)
    Cleveland I 126-127
    Loyd 12
BALON see BALLON
BALOUN see BALLON
BANASTRE
    1 (Banastre)
    3 (Banestre)
    5 (Banestre)
    7 (Robert Banastre)
    Cleveland I 124-126
BANDY
    1 & 3 (Bandy)
    Cleveland I 135-136 (=Bondy)
BANESTRE see BANASTRE
BANET see BAVENT
BANS
    8 (Raoul de Bans)
BAPAUMES
    8 (Raoul de Bapaumes)
BARBASON see BRABASON
BARBAYON see BRABASON
BARBEDOR
    1 (Barduedor)
    5 (Barbedor)
    Cleveland I 159
BARBES
    8 (Robert de Barbes)
    Rotbertus de Barbes 1086 ST
BARCHAMPE
    1 & 3 (Barchampe)
    Cleveland I 201
BARDOLF
    1 (Bardolfe)
    2 (Bardelfe)
    3 (Bardolf)
    5 (Bardolf)

29

Cleveland I 57-61
BARDUEDOR see BARBEDOR
BARET
  1 (Barrett)
  3 (Barret)
  5 (Baret)
  Cleveland I 161-162
BARNIUALE
  1 (Barniuale)
  2 (Barnevil)
  3 (Barneuale)
  Cleveland I 165-166
BARRAY see BARRY
BARRE
  1 (Barre)
  Cleveland I 150
BARRET(T) see BARET
BARREUILE
  6 (Le sire de Barreuile)
BARRY
  1 & 3 (Barry)
  5 (Barray; Barry)
  Cleveland I 167-169
BARTE
  3 (Barte)
BARY see BARRY
BASCOUN
  1 (Bascoun)
  Cleveland I 139-140
BASKERUILE
  1 (Baskeruile)
  2 (Baskarvyle)
  4 (Martels de Basquevile)
  5 (Baskerville)
  6 (Martell de Basqueuill)
  Cleveland I 83-86
  see also MARTEL
BASSET
  1 & 2 & 3 & 5 (Basset)
  7 (Osmond Basset; Raoul
    Basset; Toustain Basset)
  8 (Guillaume Basset; Raoul Basset)
  Radulfus/Ricardus/Willielmus
    Basset 1086 ST
  Cleveland I 61-66
  Loyd 12
BASTARD
  1 (Bastard)
  7 & 8 (Robert Le Bastard)
  Robertus Bastard 1086 TC
  Cleveland I 185-186
BAUDEMONT
  Loyd 12-13
BAUDEWIN
  1 (Baudewin)
  3 (Baudewine)

  5 (Baudewyn; Baudyn)
  Cleveland I 144-145
BAUDYN see BAUDEWIN
BAVENT
  1 (Banet)
  5 (Bavent)
  8 (Bavent)
  Cleveland I 108-109
  Loyd 13
BAYBOF see BRAIBOUE
BAYEUX
  1 (Baious)
  4 (L'Eveske Odun)
  5 (Baius)
  6 (Odo, Byshoppe of Baion)
  7 & 8 (Eudes, Eveque de Bayeux)
  Odo Baiocensis Episcopus
    1086 TC
Odo [the Latinised form of Eudes], Bishop of
Bayeux, afterwards Earl of Kent, the Conqueror's
half-brother, is mentioned by William of Poitiers as
being in the expeditionary force to pray, but he is
named and shown on the Bayeux Tapestry, baton in
hand, rallying the Normans who were fleeing before
the English onslaught; whether he fought against the
English army or only stopped the Normans in flight
remains doubtful. He left an illegitimate son, from
whom descended the great Norman house of Le
Hommet, hereditary constables of Normandy.
BAYLIFE see BAILIF
BAYLON see BALLON
BAYLOUN see BALLON
BAYONS
  3 (Bayons)
BEALUM see BALLON
BEAMONT see BEAUMONT
BEAUCHAMP
  1 (Beauchampe)
  2 & 3 & 5 (Beauchamp)
  7 & 8 (Hugue de Beauchamp)
  Hugo de Belcamp 1086 TC
  Cleveland I 127-133
BEAUFAULT
  6 (Le sire de Beaufault)
  Rad. de Bella Fago
    /Bello Fago 1086 TC
BEAUFITZ see BEAUUISE
BEAUFORT see BEUFORT
BEAUFOU see BELEFROUN
BEAUGIEN
  6 (Eude de Beaugien)
BEAUMAIS see BELMEIS
BEAUMEIS see BELMEIS
BEAUMONT
  1 & 2 (Beaumont)
  4 (Rogier de Belmont)

5 (Beaumont)
6 (Roger, Earle of Beamont)
7 (Robert de Beaumont)
8 (Henri de Beaumont)
Rogerius de Belmont 1086 TC
Cleveland I 145-148
Loyd 13
Robert de Beaumont, mentioned by William of Poitiers and Orderic, was undoubtedly at the Battle. He was singled out for praise by William of Poitiers. He descended from Thorold de Pontaudemer and a sister of Gunnor, Duchess of Normandy [either Aveline or Wevie; Cf. G.H. White's paper on "The Sisters and Nieces of Gunnor, Duchess of Normandy" in "The Genealogist", N.S. xxxvii, 57-65 & 128-132]. He succeeded his father Roger, as Lord of Pontaudemer and Beaumont in Normandy, and his maternal uncle as Count of Meulan in France, and was created Earl of Leicester by Henry I. From his elder son, Waleran, Count of Meulan, descended several Norman lines, whilst the second son Robert, Earl of Leicester, was grandfather of Robert, 4th Earl of Leicester, who died without issue in 1204. Roger de Beaumont was not himself at the Battle, being left in Normandy as chief adviser of the Duchess Maud.
BEAUPEL
    2 (Beaupel)
BEAUPERE
    1 (Beaupere)
    3 (Beawper)
    Cleveland I 157
BEAUPOUNT
    3 (Beaupount)
    Cleveland III 286
BEAUSON
    6 (Le sire de Beauson)
BEAUUISE
    1 (Beauuise)
    2 (Beauvys)
    8 (Goubert de Beauvais)
    Cleveland I 195 (=Beaufitz)
BEAUVAIS see BEAUUISE
BEAUVYS see BEAUUISE
BEAWPER see BEAUPERE
BEC see BEKE
BEELHELME
    1 (Beelhelme)
    3 (Belhelme)
    Cleveland I 187
BEER
    3 (Beer)
BEHUNT
    6 (Affroy de Behunt)
BEISIN
    1 (Beisin)

Cleveland I 197
BEKARD
    5 (Bekard)
BEKE
    1 & 3 (Beke)
    6 (Tostamdubec)
    7 & 8 (Geoffroi du Bec)
    Goisfridus de Bech 1086 TC
    Walterus Bec 1086 ST
    Cleveland I 120-123
BELASYSE see BELESUZ
BELEFROUN
    1 & 3 (Belefroun)
    4 (Robert sire de Belfou)
    7 (Guillaume de Beaufou;
    Robert de Beaufou)
    8 (Guillaume de Beaufou)
    Cleveland I 200-201
    (=Belfou)
BELEMIS see BELMEIS
BELENCUN
    Bernardus de Belencun'
    1086 ST
BELENERS see BELEUERS
BELESUZ
    1 (Belesuz)
    3 (Bolesur)
    3 (Belasyse)
    Cleveland I 190-191
    & III 275-278
BELET see BELLET
BELEUERS
    1 (Beleuers)
    3 (Beleners)
    Cleveland I 177-182
    (=Belvoir)
BELEVILE
    5 (Belevile)
    Cleveland III 360-361
BELEW see BELLEWE
BELFOU see BELEFROUN
BELHELME see BEELHELME
BELLA FAGO see BEAUFAULT
BELKNAPE
    3 (Belknape)
    Cleveland III 284-285
BELLAMY see BELOMY
BELLET
    1 (Bellet)
    3 (Belot)
    8 (Guillaume Belet)
    Will(i)elmus Belet/Belot
    1086 TC
    Cleveland I 143-144
BELLEWE
    1 (Bellewe)

3 & 5 (Belew)
Cleveland I 174-175
BELLIRE
1 (Bellire)
Cleveland I 184-185
BELLOMONT see BEAUMONT
BELMEIS
1 (Belemis)
7 & 8 (Richard de Beaumais)
Cleveland I 195-197
Loyd 13-14
BELMONT see BEAUMONT
BELNAI see BENNY
BELOMY
3 (Belomy)
Cleveland III 283-284
(=Bellamy)
BELOT see BELLET
BELVACO
Goisbertus de Belvaco
1086 TC
BENNY
5 (Benny)
Cleveland III 359 (=Belnai)
Loyd 14 (Belnai)
BENZ
Osmundus Benz 1086 TC
BERCHELAI
Radulfus/Rogerius de
Berchelai 1086 TC
BERCHERES
8 (Ours de Bercheres)
BERENEUILE see BURNEL
BEREVILE
Nigellus de Berevile 1086 TC
BERGOS
2 (Bergos)
BERNAI
8 (Raoul de Bernai)
Radulfus de Bernai 1086 ST
BERNERS
1 & 2 & 3 (Berners)
7 & 8 (Hugue de Bernieres)
Hugo de Berneres 1086 TC
Cleveland I 98-100
Loyd 14
BERNEVALE see BURNEL
BERNEVILE see BURNEL
BERNEVYLE see BURNEL
BERNON
1 (Bernon)
Cleveland I 197
BERRURIER
8 (Herve Le Berrurier)
BERTEUILAY see BRETTEVILLE
BERTEUILE see BRETTEVILLE

BERTIN
1 (Bertin)
3 (Bertine)
5 (Bertin)
Cleveland I 173-174
BERTIVILE see BRETEVILE
BERTRAM
1 & 2 & 3 (Bertram)
4 (Robert Bertram, torz)
5 (Bertrem)
7 (Robert Bertram le Tort;
Guillaume Bertram)
8 (Guillaume Bertran)
William de Bertram 1086 TC
Cleveland 1 47-51
BERTRAN
4 (De Peleit le
fitz Bertran)
BERVILLE
8 (Neel de Berville)
BESYLE
2 (Besyle)
BETEUILE see BRETEVILE
BEUERY
1 (Beuery)
5 (Bevery)
Cleveland I 175
BEUFORT
3 (Beufort)
Cleveland III 285-286
BEUILL
1 (Beuill)
7 (Le Sire de Beville
et d'Yvelin)
Cleveland I 157-159
(=Bovill, Boyville)
BEUNAI see BELNAI
BEUVRIERE see BEVERS
BEVERY see BEUERY
BEVERS
5 (Bevers)
7 & 8 (Dreu de La Beuvriere)
Drogo de Bevraria/Bevreire/
Bevrere 1086 TC
BEVILLE see BEUILL
BIARD see BIARS
BIARS
4 (Avenals des Biarz)
5 (Biard)
6 (Le sire de Biars;
Aue Neel de Biars)
7 (Avenel des Biards)
BIARZ see BIARS
BICKARD
1 (Bickard)
Cleveland I 123-124

32

BIDIN
  5 (Bidin)
BIENFAITE see ORBEC
BIFORD
  5 (Biford)
  Cleveland III 356BIGOT
  1 (Bigot)
  2 (Bygod)
  3 (Bigot)
  4 (L'ancestre Hue li Bigot)
  5 (Bigot)
  6 (Hue le Vigot alias Bigot
    de Maletot)
  7 (Roger Bigot, Seig. de
    Maltot; Guillaume Bigot)
  8 (Roger Bigot)
  Rogerus Bigot/Bigotus
    1086 TC & ST
  Cleveland I 66-67
  Loyd 14-15
BINGARD see BYNGARD
BYRON see BOROUN
BISET
  2 (Biset)
  Cleveland I 55-57 (=Byseg)
  Loyd 15-16
BIVILLE
  8 (Guillaume de Biville;
    Honfroi de Biville)
BLAMUILLE
  6 (Le sire de Blamuille)
BLANGI
  8 (Guimond de Blangi)
BLEYN
  5 (Bleyn)
  Cleveland III 359-360 (=Bloin)
BLOIET
  Radulfus Bloiet 1086 ST
BLOIN see BLEYN
BLON see BLUNT
BLOND see BLUNT
BLONDELL see BLUNDELL
BLONDUS see BLUNT
BLOSSEVILE
  8 (Gilbert de Blosseville)
  Gislebertus de Blosseuile
    1086 ST
BLOUET see BLUAT
BLOUNTE see BLUNT
BLUAT
  1 (Bluat)
  5 (Bluett)
  7 (Robert Blouet)
  8 (Raoul Blouet; Robert Blouet)
  Cleveland I 112-114
BLUETT see BLUAT

BLUNDEL
  1 (Blundell; Blondell)
  3 (Blundel; Blundell)
  Cleveland I 109-111
BLUNDET
  5 (Blundet; twice)
BLUNDUS see BLUNTBLUNT
  1 & 3 (Blunt)
  5 (Blounte)
  7 & 8 (Guillaume Le Blond;
    Gilbert Le Blond)
  Ro(d)bertus Blon/Blundus
    1086 TC & ST
  Willelmus Blundus 1086 TC
  Gislebertus Blon/Blondus/
    Blundus 1086 ST
  Cleveland I 152-157
BOCEIO see BUCEIO
BOCI see BUSHY
BOC UILLA
  Willelmus de Boc uilla 1086 ST
BODIN
  1 (Bodin)
  7 & 8 (Raoul Botin)
  Cleveland I 170-172
BODYT
  3 (Bodyt)
BOELS
  1 (Boels)
  3 (Bools)
  Cleveland I 197-200
BOESEVILLA see BOSVILLE
BOHON see BOHUN
BOHUN
  1 (Bohun)
  2 (Boun)
  3 (Bohun)
  4 (Onfrei de Bohon)
  5 (Boown)
  7 & 8 (Honfroi de Bohon)
  Humfr. de Bohun 1086 TC
  Cleveland I 71-76
  Loyd 16
BOIS
  1 (Bois)
  2 & 5 (Boys)
  6 (Le sire de Bois)
  7 & 8 (Guillaume du Bosc)
  8 (Hugue de Bois Hebert)
  Cleveland I 88-89
  Loyd 16-17
BOIS-ROHARD see BOSCROARD
BOISSEL
  8 (Roger Boissel)
BOLBEC see BOLEBEC
BOLEBEC

33

2 (Bolebeke)
4 (Luce de Bolbec)
6 (Hue sire de Bollebec)
7 & 8 (Hugue de Bolbec)
Hugo de Bolebec/Bolebech
1086 TC
Loyd 17
see also GIFFARD
BOLESUR see BELESUZ
BOLLEBEC see BOLEBEC
BOLLERS see BOWLERS
BOLLEVILLE see BOLVYLE
BOLVYLE
2 (Bolvyle)
7 (Le Sire de Bolleville)
BONDEUILE
1 & 3 (Bondeuile)
8 (Richard de Bondeville)
Cleveland I 81-82
BONDEVILLE see BONDEUILE
BONETT
1 (Bonett)
2 (Bonet)
5 (Bonet)
Cleveland I 166-167
BONEVIL
2 (Bonevyle)
3 (Bonuile)
BONNEBOSQ see BONNESBOZ
BONNESBOZ
4 (Sire de Bonnesboz)
7 (Le Sire de Bonnebosq)
BONRETT
1 (Bonrett)
5 (Bourte)
Cleveland I 162-163
BONVALEST
8 (Guillaume Bonvalet)
Willelmus Bonvalest
/Buenvaslest
/Bonuaslet 1086 TC & ST
BONVALET see BONVALEST
BONUEIER
1 (Bonueier)
Cleveland I 183-184
BONUILE see BONEVIL
BONYLAYNE see BOUNILAINE
BOOLS see BOELS
BOOWN see BOHUN
BORANUILE
1 (Boranuile)
Cleveland I 176-177
BORARD see BOSCROARD
BORCI
Serlo Borci 1086 ST
BORDINEIO

Loyd 18
BOROUN
5 (Boroun)
Cleveland III 357-359
(reading Biroune=Byron)
BOSC see BOIS
BOSCNORMAN
8 (Roger de Bosc Normand)
Rogerus de Boscnorman
1086 TC
BOSCO see BAUDEMONT and BOIS
BOSCHERVILLE
Loyd 19
BOSCROARD
7 (Le Sire de Bosc-Roard)
8 (Guillaume de Bosc Roard;
Roger de Bosc Roard)
Willielmus de Boscroard
1086 ST
Loyd 18-19
BOSC-ROHARD see BOSCROARD
BOSKERVILLE see BOSCHERVILLE
BOSVILLE
1 (Busseuile)
3 (Busseuile)
5 (Boseville)
Cleveland I 150-152
Loyd 19
BOTECOURT see BUTTECOURT
BOTELER
1 (Boteler; Botelere)
2 & 3 & 5 (Boteler)
Cleveland I 89-94
BOTERELL
2 (Boterell)
BOTES
2 (Botes)
BOTETOUR
2 (Botetour)
BOTEUILE see BOTEVILE
BOTEVILAIN see BOUTEVILAIN
BOTEVILE
1 (Boteuile)
2 (Botevyle)
3 (Botuile)
Cleveland I 184
BOTIN see BODIN
BOTTELER see BOTELER
BOTUILE see BOTEVILE
BOULOGNE
Eustache, Comte de Boulogne
Eustace, Count of Boulogne, mentioned by
William of Poitiers and Orderic and named on
the Bayeux Tapestry, was undoubtedly at the
Battle. He was son of Eustace I and had married
Godgifu, sister of Edward the Confessor and

34

widow of Dreu, Count of the French Vexin [Their son, Walter, Count of the French Vexin, and his wife Biota of Maine, were captured by William of Normandy in his Maine campaign and taken to Falaise, where they were promptly poisoned by their genial host; for, as G.H. White said, the Conqueror was a retail, as well as a wholesale, butcher]. By his second wife, Ida, who brought him Bouillon, he had, with other children, the famous Godfrey of Bouillon. In the next century Boulogne became for a time attached to England, through the marriage of the heiress to King Stephen.

BOUN see BOHUN
BOUNDES
   1 (Boundes)
   Cleveland I 138-139
BOUNILAINE
   1 (Bounilaine)
   3 (Bonylayne)
BOUNDEVILLE
   5 (Boundeville)
BOURCHER
   1 (Bourcher)
   Cleveland I 94-98
BOURDET see BURDET
BOURGUIGNON
   8 (Fouque Le Bourguignon)
BOURNEVILLE see BURNEL
BOURTE see BONRETT
BOUTEVILAIN
   2 (Bouteveleyn)
   4 (Botevilain)
   5 (Buttevillain)
   7 (Le Sire de
     Bouttevillain)
   Cleveland I 87-88
BOWLERS
   3 (Bowlers)
   Cleveland III 281 (=Bollers)
BOWSER
   3 (Bowser)
   Cleveland III 278 (=Bourchier)
BOYS see BOIS
BOYVILE
   5 (Boyvile)
BRA see BRAY
BRABANSON see BRABASON
BRABASON
   1 (Brabason; Brabaion)
   3 (Barbason; Barbayon)
   5 (Brabasoun)
   7 (Jacques Le Brabancon)
   Cleveland I 82-83
BRACY
   1 & 5 (Bracy)

   6 (Le sire de Bracy)
   7 (Le Seigneur de Brecey)
   Cleveland I 136-138
BRAEHUS
   3 (Braehus)
BRAI see BRAY
BRAIBOF see BRAIBOUE
BRAIBOUE
   1 (Braibuf)
   2 (Braybuffe) 3 (Braybuf)
   5 (Baybof)
   8 (Hugue de Brebeuf)
   Hugo de Braiboue 1086 ST
   Cleveland I 100-101
   Loyd 19-20
BRAINE
   1 (Braine)
   Cleveland I 187-188
BRAIOSA see BRIOUZE
BRAND(E)
   1 (Brande)
   3 (Brand)
   5 (Braund)
   Willielmus Brant 1086 ST
   Cleveland I 101-102
BRASARD
   1 & 3 (Brasard)
   Cleveland I 186-187
   (=Busard)
BRAUNCH(E)
   1 (Braunch)
   3 (Braunche)
   Cleveland I 101-106
BRAUND see BRAND
BRAUNZ
   2 (Braunz)
BRAY
   1 (Bray)
   2 (Bra)
   5 (Bray)
   6 (Hugh de Gournay
     sire le de Bray)
   7 & 8 (Guillaume de Brai)
   Cleveland I 133-135
BRAYBUF see BRAIBOUE
BRAYEN
   6 (Hamon de Brayen)
BREANTE
   6 (Le sire de Breante)
BREBEUF see BRAIBOUE
BREBUS
   1 (Brebus)
   Cleveland I 52-55
BRECEY see BRACY
BREICOURT
   5 (Breicourt)

Cleveland III 360
? see also BRUCOURT
BRENALL
  6 (Le sire de Brenall)
BRENCON
  6 (Le sire de Brencon)
BRENT
  1 (Brent)
  Cleveland I 188-189
BRET see BRETTE
BRETEUIL see BRETTEVILLE
BRETTE
  1 (Brette)
  3 (Bret)
  Cleveland I 159-161
BRETTEVILLE
  1 (Beteuile; Berteuilay)
  3 (Berteuile; Bertevyley)
  4 (Guillaume fils
    Osber de Bretuil)
  5 (Bretevile; twice)
  7 & 8 (Roger de Breteuil;
    Gilbert de Bretteville)
  Gislebertus de Bretevile
    1086 TC & ST
  Bretel 1086 ST
  Cleveland I 172-173
  see also FitzOSBERN
BRETON(N)
  1 & 3 (Breton)
  5 (Bretonn)
  7 & 8 (Auvrai Le Breton)
  Cleveland I 111-112
BRETUIL see BRETTEVILLE
BREUIL
  8 (Osberne du Breuil)
BREUS see BRUCE
BREVES see BRUCE
BREWES see BRIOUZE
BRIAN see BRYAN
BRIANSOUN
  5 (Briansoun)
  Cleveland III 359
BRIENCORT
  4 (Sire de Briencort)
BRIMOV
  8 (Renier de Brimou)
  Rainerus de Brimov 1086 TC
BRIOUZE
  2 (Brewes)
  7 & 8 (Guillaume de Briouse)
  Willelmus de Braiosa 1086 TC
  Cleveland I 52-55
  Loyd 20
BRIQUEVILLE
  8 (De Briqueville)

BRITTANY
  4 (Alainz Ferganz)
  6 (Alan sergent Counte
    de Britaigne)
  7 (Alain Fergant,
    Comte de Bretagne)
BRIT(T)O
  Aluredus/Gotzelinus/Maigno/
    Ogerus/Rainaldus/
    Waldinus Brito 1086 TC
  Tihellus Britto 1086 TC
BRIX
  7 & 8 (Robert de Brix)
BROILEM
  1 (Broilem)
  Cleveland I 140
BROILG
  1 (Browe)
  5 (Broy)
  Osbernus/Osbertus de Broilg
    1086 ST
  Cleveland I 177
  Loyd 20-21
BROLEUY
  1 (Broleuy)
  Cleveland I 140
BROMEVILE
  5 (Bromevile)
BRONCE see BRUCE
BROTH
  5 (Broth)
BROUNE see BROWNE
BROWE see BROILG
BROWNE
  1 (Browne)
  3 (Broune)
  Cleveland I 114-120
BROY see BROILG
BROYLEBY
  3 (Broyleby)
BRUCE
  1 (Bronce)
  1 (Brutz)
  2 (Brus)
  5 (Bruys; twice)
  Robertus de Bruis 1086 TC
  Cleveland I 102-105
BRUCOURT
  7 (Le Sire de Brucourt)
  ? see also BREICOURT
BRUIERE
  8 (Raoul de La Bruiere)
BRUNETOT
  6 (Le sire de Brunetot)
BRUTZ see BRUCE
BRUYS see BRUCE

BRYAN
1 (Bryan)
5 (Brian)
Cleveland I 169-170
BUCEIO
Loyd 21
BUCI see BUSHY
BUDI
8 (Gilbert de Budi)
Gislebertus de Budi 1086 TC
BUENVASLEST see BONVALEST
BUFFARD
1 & 3 (Buffard)
Cleveland I 182-183
BUILLI see BUSLIBUILLOU
6 (Bandonni of Buillou)
BULLI see BUSLI
BULLEBEK see BOLEBEC
BULMERE
3 (Bulmere)
Cleveland III 278-281
BURCI
7 & 8 (Serlon de Burci)
Serlo de Burci 1086 TC
BURDET
1 & 3 & 5 (Burdet)
7 (Robert Bourdet)
8 (Hugue Bourdet; Robert Bourdet)
Hugo Burdet 1086 ST
Robertus Burdet 1086 ST
Cleveland I 191-194
BURDON
1 & 3 (Burdon)
5 (Burdoun)
Cleveland I 148-150
BURES
1 & 3 (Bures)
7 (Michel de Bures)
Cleveland I 86
BURGENOU
2 (Burgenou)
BURGH
1 & 3 & 5 (Burgh)
Cleveland I 105-106
BURNEL
1 (Burnell; Bereneuile)
2 (Bernevyle)
3 (Burnel)
5 (Burnel; Bernevale;
    Bernevile)
7 & 8 (Guillaume de Bourneville)
Nigellus de Berevile 1086 TC
Willielmus de Burneuilla/
    Burnoluilla/Burnouilla
    1086 ST
Cleveland I 140-143, 174

? see also BORANUILE
BURNEVILLE see BURNEL
BURON see BURUN
BURS
2 (Burs)
BURSIGNI
8 (Guillaume de Bursigni)
Willielmus de Bursigni
    1086 ST
BURUN
8 (Erneis de Buron)
Emegis/Erneis/Radulfus
    de Burun 1086 TC
BUSARD
5 (Busard)
Cleveland I 186-187
BUSCEL
1 (Busshell)
3 (Buschell)
5 (Buscel)
Rogerus Buissel 1086 ST
Cleveland I 175-176
BUSHY
1 (Bushy)
3 (Busshy)
5 (Bussy)
7 & 8 (Robert de Buci)
Robertus de Boci/Buci
    1086 TC & ST
Cleveland I 106-108
BUSLI
8 (Roger de Bulli)
Rogerus de Busli 1086 TC
BUSSEUILE see BOSVILLE
BUTTECOURT
1 & 3 (Buttecourt)
5 (Buttencourt)
Cleveland I 51-52
BUTTEVILLAIN see BOUTEVILAIN
BVIVILE
Hunfridus de Bvivile 1086 TC
BYGOD see BIGOT
BYGORE
Loyd 21-22
BYNGARD
5 (Byngard)
BYRON see BIROUNE
BYSEG
1 & 3 (Byseg)
Cleveland I 55-57 (=Bisset)
CADOMO
Galterus seu Walterus
    de Cadomo/Gadomo
    1086 ST
CADURCIS see CHAWORTH
CAEN

37

7 (Gautier de Caen)
8 (Fouque de Caen; Maurin de Caen)
CAHAGNES
    4 (De Chaaignes)
    7 & 8 (Guillaume de Cahaignes)
    Willelmus de Cahainges
      1086 TC & ST
    Loyd 52 (Cahagnes/Keynes)
CAHAIGNES see CAHAGNES
CAHAINGES see CAHAGNES
CAILGI see CAILLY
CAILLIE see CAILLY
CAILLY
    4 (Seignor de Caillie)
    6 (Le sire de Cailly)
    7 & 8 (Guillaume de Cailly)
    Willelmus Cailgi 1086 TC
    Loyd 22 (Cailli)
CAIRON see CARON
CAISNETO see CHESNEY
CALCEIS
    Loyd 22-23
CAMBRAI see CAMBREIS
CAMBREIS
    4 (Cil de Combrai)
    6 (Le sire de Cambray)
    7 (Geoffroi de Combray)
    8 (Geoffroi Cambrai)
    Godefridus de Cambrai 1086 TC
    Loyd 23
CAMEVILLE see CAMUILLE
CAMIN see CAMNINE
CAMMILE see CAMUILLE
CAMMOIS see CAMOIS
CAMNINE
    3 (Camnine)
    Cleveland III 290 (=Camin)
CAMOIS
    1 (Camois)
    2 (Cammois)
    3 (Camos)
    5 (Camoys)
    Cleveland I 201-203
CAMPEAUX
    Loyd 23
CAMPELLIS see CAMPEAUX
CAMPO ARNULFI
    Loyd 26
CAMPO FLORE
    Loyd 26
CAMPO FLORIDO
    Loyd 27
CAMUILLE
    1 (Cammile; Camuille)
    3 (Chanuille)
    5 (Cameville)

Cleveland I 203-205, 270-271
CANDOS see CHANDOS
    7 (Le Sire de Canouville)
CANOUVILLE
    8 (De Canouville)
CANTELON see CANTELOU
CANTELOU
    1 (Chantelow)
    2 (Cantelou)
    3 (Chantilowe)
    5 (Cauntelow)
    Cleveland I 237-241
    (=Cantilupe)
    Loyd 24
CANTEMOR
    2 (Cantemor)
CANVILE see CAMUILLE
CAPEROUN
    1 (Caperoun)
    Cleveland I 256-257
CARBONELL
    1 (Carbonelle)
    3 (Carbonell)
    7 (Hugue de Carbonnel)
    8 (Carbonnel)
    Carbonel 1086 TC
    Cleveland I 251-252
CARDON/CARDUN
    8 (Guillaume de Cardon)
    Willielmus Cardon/Cardun
      1086 ST
CAREUILE
    1 (Careuile)
    2 (Carvyle; Cavervyle)
    Cleveland I 250-251
CAREW
    3 (Carew)
CARI
    2 (Cari)
CARICURIA see CHEVERCOURT
CARLEVILLE
    Loyd 25
CARNET
    8 (Guillaume de Carnet)
CARNOT
    Radulfus Carnot'
      1086 TC & SC
CARON
    2 (Caroun)
    8 (Guillaume de Cairon)
    Willielmus de Caron/Carun
      1086 ST
    Loyd 25
CAROUN see CARON
CARTAICT see CATERAY
CARTERAI see CATERAY

CARTERET see CATERAY
CARTRAI see CATERAY
CARUN see CARON
CARVYLE see CAREUILE
CASTELLON
  8 (Guillaume de Castillon)
  Willielmus de Castellon
    1086 ST
  Loyd 25
CASTILLON see CASTELLON
CATERAY
  1 & 3 (Cateray)
  4 (Onfrei de Cartrai;
    Maugier de Carterai
    novel chevalier)
  5 (Tarteray)
  6 (Affroy & Mauigr de
    Cartaict)
  7 (Honfroi de Carteret;
    Mauger de Carteret)
  8 (Honfroi de Carteret;
    Mauger de Carteret;
    Roger de Carteret)
  Cleveland I 266-269
    (=Carteret)
  Loyd 25 (Carteret)
CAUCEIS see CALCEIS
CAUNTELOW see CANTELOU
CAVERVYLE see CAREUILE
CEAUCE
  8 (Guillaume de Ceauce)
CESARIS BURGUM see CHERBOURG
CHAAIGNES see CAHAGNES
CHAITERS
  1 (Chaiters)
  3 (Chayters)
  Cleveland I 262 (=Chartres)
CHALERS
  2 (Chalers)
CHALLEYS
  2 (Scales)
  5 (Challeys)
  7 (Le Sire d'Escalles)
  8 (Hardouin d'Ecalles)
  Harduinus de Scalers 1086 TC
  Harduinus de Escalers 1086 ST
  Cleveland III 362-365
    (=Scales)
CHALLOUNS
  5 (Challouns)
  Cleveland III 362
CHAMBERAYE
  1 (Chamberaye)
  Cleveland I 241-242
    (=Cambrai)
CHAMBERLAINE

  1 & 3 (Chamberlaine)
  2 (Chaumburleys)
  5 (Chaumberlayn)
  Cleveland I 210-211
CHAMBERNOUNE see CHAMPERNOWNE
CHAMBURNOUN see CHAMPERNOWNE
CHAMPAGNE see CHAMPAIN
CHAMPAIN
  1 (Champaine)
  3 (Champain)
  7 & 8 (Eudes, Comte de Champagne)
  Cleveland I 249-250
CHAMPENEY see CHAMPNEY
CHAMPERNOWNE
  1 (Chamburnoun)
  2 (Chaumbursoun)
  3 (Chambernoune)
  5 (Chaumberoun)
  Cleveland I 211
  Loyd 26
CHAMPEUS see CAMPEAUX
CHAMPNEY
  1 (Champney)
  3 (Champeney)
  5 (Champeneys)
  Cleveland I 247-249
CHANCER
  3 (Chancer)
  Cleveland III 291-294 (=Chaucer)
CHANCEUS
  5 (Chanceus)
  Cleveland III 361-362
CHANCY see CHAUNCY
CHANDOS see CHAUNDOS
CHANFLEUR
  Loyd 27
CHANTELOW see CANTELOU
CHANTILOWE see CANTELOU
CHANUILLE see CAMUILLE
CHAORCIIS see CHAWORTH
CHAPES
  1 (Chopis)
  5 (Chapes)
  Cleveland I 235 (=Chopis)
CHAREBERGE see CHERBOURG
CHARLES
  1 & 3 (Charles)
  Cleveland I 252
CHARTRAI see CARTERET
CHARTRES
  5 (Chartres)
  8 (Raoul de Chartres)
  see also CHAITERS
CHARY
  2 (Chary)
CHAUCER see CHANCER

39

CHAUDUT
2 & 5 (Chaudut)
CHAUMBERLAYN see CHAMBERLAINE
CHAUMBEROUN see CHAMPERNOWNE
CHAUMBURLEYS see CHAMBERLAINE
CHAUMBURSOUN see CHAMPERNOWNE
CHAUMONT
1 & 5 (Chaumont)
3 (Chawmont)
Cleveland I 254-256
CHAUNCY
1 & 5 (Chauncy)
3 (Chancy)
Cleveland I 205-207
CHAUNDOS
1 (twice; Chaundos)
3 (Chaundos)
5 (Chaundoys)
7 (Robert de Chandos)
8 (Robert de Chandos;
Roger de Chandos)
Rogerus de Candos 1086 ST
Cleveland I 223-229
Loyd 26-27
CHAUNDUIT 1 (Chaunduit)
3 (Chaunduyt)
Cleveland I 235-237
CHAUNUILE
3 (Chaunuile)
CHAVENT see CHAWENT
CHAWARD
2 & 5 (Chaward)
CHAWENT
1 & 3 (Chawent)
5 (Chavent)
Cleveland I 205
CHAWMONT see CHAUMONT
CHAWNES
1 (Chawnes; Chawnos)
3 (Chawnes; Chawnos)
Cleveland I 253-254
CHAWNOS see CHAWNES
CHAWORTH
1 (Chaworth)
3 (Chaworthe)
Cleveland I 229-233
Loyd 27
CHAYMES
6 (Le Bisquams de Chaymes)
CHAYTERS see CHAITERS
CHEINE see CHESNEY
CHEINES see CHESNEY
CHENIL
5 (Chenil)
Cleveland I 265-266
(=Cheynell)

CHERBOURG
1 (Chereberge)
3 (Chareberge)
8 (Anquetil de Cherbourg)
Cleveland I 252-253
Loyd 27
CHERCOURT see CHERECOURT
CHEREBERGE see CHERBOURG
CHERECOURT
1 & 3 (Cherecourt)
5 (Chercourt)
Cleveland I 269-270
(=Chevercourt)
Loyd 28 (Chevercourt)
CHERNET
Willielmus de Chernet 1086 ST
CHESNEY
1 (Cheine; Cheines)
2 (Cheyne)
3 (Cheyne; Cheynes)
5 (Cheyni)
Radulfus de Caisned 1086 ST
Cleveland I 257-259
and 265-266 (=Cheynell)
Loyd 27-28
CHESTER, Earls of   Loyd 28
CHEVERCOURT see CHERECOURT
CHEVRE
7 (Guillaume La Chievre)
8 (Guillaume La Chevre)
Willielmus Cheure 1086 ST
Willelmus Chievre 1086 TC
CHEYNE(S) see CHESNEY
CHEYNI see CHESNEY
CHIEVRE see CHEVRE
CHIRAY
Loyd 28-29
CHOKES
Loyd 29
CHOLMELEY
1 (Cholmeley)
3 (Cholmelay)
Cleveland I 247
CHOPIS see CHAPES
CIERREIO see CHIRAY
CINTHEAUX
4 (Cil de Sainteals)
6 (Le sire de Sainteaulx)
7 (Le Sire de Cintheaux)
CIOCHES
7 (Gonfroi de Cioches)
8 (Gonfroi de Cioches;
Sigar de Cioches)
Gunfridus de Cioches 1086 TC
Sigar de Cioches 1086 TC
CLARAUS

2 (Claraus)
CLAREL
  1 & 3 (Clarell)
  2 & 5 (Clarel)
  Cleveland I 234-235
CLARELL see CLAREL
CLAREMAUS see CLERVAUX
CLARVAILE see CLERVAUX
CLARUAYS
  1 (Clerenay)
  3 (Clereney; Claruays)
  Cleveland I 271-275 & III 290
CLAVILLA
  1 (Clinels)
  2 (Clevyle)
  8 (Fouque de Claville)
  Walterus de Clavile 1086 TC
  Cleveland I 277-278
    (=Cliville)
  Loyd 29
  see also CLERVAUX
CLAVILLE see CLAVILLA
CLERA see CLERE
CLERE
  6 (Le sire de Clere)
  Loyd 29
CLEREVALX see CLERVAUX
CLERMOUNT
  2 (Clermount)
CLERVAUX
  1 (Cleremaus)
  3 (Claremaus; Claruaile)
  5 (Clerevalx)
  Cleveland I 233-234 & III 294-
    296 (=Claville)
CLEVILE see CLAVILLA
CLIFFORD
  1 (Clifford)
  3 (Clyfford)
  Cleveland I 278
CLINCHAMPS
  7 (Le Sire de Clinchamps)
  8 (De Clinchamps)
CLINELS see CLAVILLA
CLINTON
  Loyd 30
CLIVILLE see CLAVILLA
COCI
  Albericus de Coci 1086 ST
COIGNERS
  5 (Coigners)
  7 (Robert de Coignieres)
COIGNIERES see COIGNERS
COLET
  3 (Colet)
  Cleveland III 290-291

COLEVILLE
  1 (Coluile)
  2 (Colevyle)
  3 (Coluile)
  5 (Colleville)
  7 & 8 (Guillaume de Colleville;
    Gilbert de Colleville)
  Gislebertus de Colauilla
    1086 ST
  Willielmus de Colevile
    1086 ST
  Cleveland I 207-210
  Loyd 30
COLLEVILLE see COLEVILLE
COLOMBELLES
  8 (Renouf de Colombelles)
COLOMBIERES see COLUMBIERS
COLUMBER see COLUMBIERS
COLUMBIERS
  1 (Columber)
  2 (Columber)
  4 (Willame de Columbieres)
  5 (Columber)
  6 (Guilliam de Colombiers)
  7 (Guillaume de Colombieres)
  8 (Baudoin de Colombieres;
    Raoul de Colombieres)
  Rannulfus de Columbels
    1086 TC & ST
  Radulfus de Columbers
    1086 ST
  Cleveland I 216-217
  Loyd 30
COLUILE see COLEVILLE
COLUNCES
  Loyd 30
COMBRAI see CAMBREIS
COMBRAY see CAMBREIS
COMIN
  1 (Comin)
  5 (Comyn)
  7 (Robert de Comines)
  Cleveland I 212-216
COMINES see COMIN
COMIUILE
  1 (Comiuile)
  Cleveland I 249 (=Conovile)
CONCHES
  4 (Raol de Conches)
  see also TESSON
CONDERAY
  1 (Conderay)
  2 (Coudree)
  3 (Couderay)
  5 (Coudray)
  Cleveland I 207

CONELL
  3 (Conell)
CONESTABLE see CONSTABLE
CONIERS
  3 (Coniers)
  Cleveland III 286-290
CONSTABLE
  1 (Conestable)
  3 & 5 (Constable)
  Cleveland I 245-247
CONSTANCES see COUTANCE
CONTEVILLE
  8 (Raoul de Conteville)
  Loyd 31-32
COQ
  7 (Alric Le Coq)
CORBET
  1 (Corbett)
  2 & 3 (Corbet)
  5 (Gorbet)
  7 (Corbet Le Normand)
  8 (Robert Corbet; Roger Corbet)
  Rogerus Corbet 1086 ST
  Cleveland I 219-223
CORBINE
  1 & 3 (Corbine)
  5 (Corby)
  8 (Guillaume Corbon;
    Hugue de Corbon)
  Hugo de Corbun 1086 ST
  Cleveland I 219 (=Corbin)
  Loyd 32 (Corbun)
CORBON see CORBINE
CORBUN see CORBINE
CORBY see CORBINE
CORCELLE
  8 (Robert de Courcelles)
  Rogerius de Corcel/Corcelle/
    Curcelle/Corcelles/
    Cvrcelles 1086 TC & ST
  Loyd 33
CORCIE see CURCY
CORLEUILE
  3 (Corleuile)
  Cleveland III 294
CORMEILLES
  8 (Ansfroi de Cormeilles;
    Goscelin de Cormeilles)
  Gozelinus/Ansfridus de
    Cormelies/Cormeliis
    1086 TC
  Loyd 33-34
CORMELIIS see CORMEILLES
CORNIOLE
  Willelmus Corniole 1086 TC
COUBRAY

  5 (Coubray)
COUCI see COUCY
COUCY
  3 (Coucy)
  7 & 8 (Aubri de Couci)
COUDERAY see CONDERAY
COUDRAY see CONDERAY
· COUDREE see CONDERAY
COUILLE
  1 (Couille)
  Cleveland I 262
COURBEPINE see CURBESPINE
COURCELLES see CORCELLE
COURCI see CURCY
COURCON see CURZON
COURCY see CURCY
COURSON see CURZON
COURSOUN see CURZON
COURTENAY
  1 (Courteney; Curtenay)
  2 (Courtnay)
  3 & 5 (Courteny)
  Cleveland I 244-245
COURTEVILE
  5 (Courtevile)
COURTNAY see COURTENAY
COUTANCES see MOWBRAY
COUVERT see COVERT
COVERT
  7 (Le Sire de Couvert)
  Loyd 67-68
COYNALE
  2 (Coynale)CRAON
  8 (Gui de Craon)
  Wido de Credun 1086 TC
  Loyd 34
CRASMESNIL
  Loyd 34
CRASSUS
  Normannus Crassus 1086 TC
CRATEL
  Godricus Cratel 1086 TC
CREDONIO see LAON
CREDUN see CRAON
CREISSI see CRESSY
CRESCY see CRESSY
CRESPIN
  4 (Willame Crespin)
  6 (Guilliam Crespin)
  7 (Guillaume Crispin,
    1er Comte du Vexin;
    Mile Crispin;
    Gilbert Crispin, 2e
    Seigneur de Tillieres)
  8 (Mile Crespin)
  Milo Crispin 1086 TC

CRESSIMERA
  Loyd 34
CRESSY
  1 & 2 & 3 (Cressy)
  5 (Crescy)
  Cleveland I 242-244
  Loyd 35
CREUECURE see CREVEQUER
CREUN see CRAON
CREUQUERE see CREVEQUER
CREVECOEUR see CREVEQUER
CREVECORT see CREVEQUER
CREVECUIR see CREVEQUER
CREVEQUEL see CREVEQUER
CREVEQUER
  1 (Creuquere)
  2 (Crevequel)
  4 (Sire de Crievecoer)
  5 (Grevequer)
  6 (Le sire Creuecure)
  7 (Robert de Crevecoeur;
    Hamon Le Seneschal)
  Cleveland I 217-219
  Loyd 35
CRIBETT
  1 (Cribett)
  3 (Cribet)
  Cleveland I 217
CRIEVECOER see CREVEQUER
CRIKETOT
  Loyd 36
CRISPIN see CRESPIN
CROC
  8 (Renaud Croc)CRUEL
  1 (Estriels; Kiriell)
  2 (Cryel)
  3 (Escriols; Kyriell)
  5 (Kyriel)
  8 (Robert Cruel)
  Robertus Cruel 1086 ST
  Cleveland II 11-15
  Loyd 36
CRUS
  2 (Crus)
CRYEL see CRUEL
CUALLIE see CUELAI
CUELAI
  1 (Cuily)
  8 (Honfroi de Culai)
  Cleveland I 276-277
  Loyd 36
CUILY see CUELAI
CUL DE LOUP
  8 (Eude Cul de Loup)
CULAI see CUELAI
CURBESPINE

  8 (Raoul de Courbepine)
  Radulfus de Curbespine
  1086 TC & ST
CURBUN see CORBUN
CURCELLE see CORCELLE
CURCI see CURCY
CURCY
  2 (Courcy)
  4 (Cil de Corcie; twice)
  7 (Richard de Courci)
  8 (Richard de Courcy)
  Ricardus de Curci 1086 TC
  Loyd 36
CURLY
  1 & 3 (Curly)
  Cleveland I 275-276
CURSEN see CURZON
CURSON see CURZON
CURTENAY see COURTENAY
CURZON
  1 (Curson)
  3 (Cursen)
  5 (Coursoun)
  7 (Robert de Courson)
  8 (Robert de Courcon)
  Robertus de Curcon/Curcun
  1086 ST
  Cleveland I 259-262
  Loyd 37
CUSSY
  7 (Le Sire de Cussy)
  8 (De Cussy)
CUVERT
  Loyd 67-68
CVRCELLES see CORCELLE
DABERNOUNE see ABERNON
DABITOT see ABETOT
DAIVILE
  Cleveland I 278-281
  Loyd 37
DAIVILLA see DAIVILE
DAKENY see AKENY
DALMARI see AMORY
DAMARY see AMORY
DAMAY see AMAY
DAMBELTON
  1 (Dambelton)
  Cleveland I 352 (=Hamilton)
DAMBEMARE
  6 (Le sire Dambemare)
DAMBLEUILLE
  6 (Eustace Dambleuille)
DAMNON
  6 (Le sire de Damnon)
DAMNOT
  1 (Damnot)

43

Cleveland I 341 (=D'Amiot)
DAMOT
  5 (Damot)
DANBINALE
  6 (Le Counte Thomas
    Danbinale)
DANCOURT
  6 (Le sire de Dancourt)
DANIEL
  1 (Daniell)
  3 (Daniel)
  7 (Roger Daniel)
  8 (Daniel)
  Cleveland I 291-292
    (=Danyers)
DANNEVILLE
  8 (Danneville)
DANVERS see DAUERS
DANVEY see ANUAY
DANWAY see ANUAY and AUFFAY
DAPISOUN
  2 (Dapisoun)
DARCY see ARCY
DARELL
  1 & 3 & 5 (Darell)
  Cleveland I 303-308
DARIE
  6 (Le sire du vall Darie)
DARQUES see ARQUES
DAUBEGNY see AUBIGNY
DAUBENAY see AUBIGNY
DAUBENY see AUBIGNY
DAUEROS see DEVEREUX
DAUERS
  1 & 3 (Dauers)
  Cleveland I 299-302
    (=Danvers)DAUMERAI
  8 (Guillaume de Daumerai)
DAUNCY
  6 (Le sire Dauncy)
DAUNDEVYLE
  2 (Daundevyle)
DAUNDON
  2 (Daundon)
DAUNGERS
  2 (Daungers)
DAUNTRE
  1 & 3 (Dauntre)
  5 (Dautre)
  Cleveland I 317-318
    (=Dawtrey/Hawtrey)
DAUONGE see AVRANCHES
DAUTRE see DAUNTRE
DAVERENGES see AVRANCHES
DAVIDIS VILLA see DAIVILE
DAYVYLE see DEUILE

DEAUUILE see DENAUILE
DEDEN
  6 (Le Counte Deden)
DEHENSE see de HEWSE
DEINCOURT see AINCOURT
DELABER
  1 (Delaber)
  3 (Delabere)
  Cleveland I 308-310
DELAHAY
  4 (Sire de la Haie)
  5 (Delahay)
  6 (Le sire de la Haye)
  7 (Eudes Le Seneschal,
    Sire de la Haie)
  Cleveland III 366-370 (=Hay)
  Loyd 51 (Haye)
DELAHILL
  1 (Delahill)
  3 (de la Hill)
  Cleveland I 311-312
DELAHOID
  1 (Delahoid)
  Cleveland I 332-333
    (=de la Hyde)
DELALINDE
  1 (Delalinde)
  3 (de la Lind)
  Cleveland I 310-311
DELAPLANCH
  1 (Delaplanch)
  3 (de la Planch)
  Cleveland I 341-342
DELAPOLE
  1 (Delapole)
  3 & 5 (de la Pole)
  Cleveland I 310
DELATOUN 5 (Delatoun)
  Cleveland III 370-371
    (=de la Doune)
DELAUACHE
  1 (Delauache)
  3 (de la Watche)
  Cleveland I 315-317
DELAUERE see VERE
DELAUND
  1 (Delaund)
  Cleveland I 334-337
DELAWARD
  1 (Ward; Delaward)
  3 (Warde; de la Warde)
  5 (Warde)
  Cleveland I 337-341
    (=de la Ward)
DELAWARE
  1 (Delaware)

5 (De la War)
Cleveland I 312-315
DELEE
1 (Delee)
Cleveland I 334
(=Lee or Ley)
DENAUILLE
1 (Denauille)
3 (Deauuile)
Cleveland I 278-281
(=Daivile)
see also DAIVILE
DENISE
1 (Denise)
3 (Denyse)
5 (Denyas)
Cleveland I 292-293
DENOIERS
Willielmus Denoiers/Denomore
/Denuers 1086 ST
DENOMORE see DENOIERS
DENUERS see DENOIERS
DENYAS see DENISE
DENYSE see DENISE
DEPEIZ
Guerno Depeiz 1086 ST
DERCY
1 & 3 (Dercy)
Cleveland I 281
DESPENSER see DISPENCER
DESYVYLE
2 (Desyvyle)
DESNY
1 (Desny)
3 (Desuye)
5 (Diseney)
Cleveland I 318-320
(=Disney)
DESTRAUNGES
5 (Destraunges)
DESUYE see DESNY
DEUAUS see VAUS
DEUILE
1 (Deuile)
2 (Dayvyle)
5 (Deyville)
Cleveland I 343
see also DOIUILE
DEUREUX
6 (Le Counte Deureux)
DEVERELLE
5 (Deverelle)
Cleveland III 365-366
DEVEREUX
1 & 3 (Daveros)
2 (Deverois; Deverouge;

Deverous)
5 (Deveroys)
Cleveland I 323-328
DEVEROIS see DEVEREUX
DEVEROUGE see DEVEREUX
DEVEROUS see DEVEREUX
DEVEROYS see DEVEREUX
DEYNCOURT see AINCOURT
DEYVILLE see DEUILE
DINAN
4 (Sire de Dinan)
DINE see DIVE
DISARD
1 & 3 (Disard)
5 (Disart)
Cleveland I 343
DISART see DISARD
DISENEY see DESNY
DISPENCER
1 (Dispencere)
3 (Dispencer; Le Despenser)
5 (Dispencer)
7 (Robert Le Despensier)
8 (Guillaume Le Despensier;
Robert Le Despensier)
Robertus Dispensator
1086 TC & ST
Willielmus Dispensator
1086 ST
DIURY see DRURY
DIVA see DIVE
DIVE
1 (Dive)
3 (Dine)
8 (Beuselin de Dives)
Cleveland I 281-283
Loyd 37
DIVES see DIVE
DOAI see DOWAI
DODINGSELS
1 (Dodingsels) 3 (Doningsels)
5 (Dodingle)
Cleveland I 302-303
DOIUILE
1 (Doiuile)
Cleveland I 343-344
(=Doynell)
see also DEUILE
DOL
8 (Hugue de Dol)
DOMFRONT
7 (Henri de Domfront)
DOMMOUN
2 (Dommoun)
DOMNOMEDARDO see DUMARD
DONINGSELS see DODINGSELS

45

DONNEBANT
  6 (Le sire Donnebant)
DONNEBOS
  6 (Le sire de Donnebos)
DONNEMCHNI
  6 (Richart Donnemchni)
DONUILLER
  6 (Le sire Donuiller)
DORBEC see ORBEC
DORENY
  5 (Doreny)
DORMAL
  6 (Le sire de Dormal)
DOUAI see DOWAI
DOULLY see DOYLY
de la DOUNE see DELATOUN
DOWAI
  8 (Fouque de Douai;
    Goscelin de Douai)
  Walscinus de Dowai 1086 ST
  Walscinus de Dwai 1086 TC
  Walterus de Doai 1086 TC
  Walterus de Dowai 1086 TC
DOWNFREVYLE
  2 (Downfrevyle)
DOYLY
  1 (Duilby)
  4 (Cil d'Oillie)
  5 (Dulee; Duylly)
  6 (Le sire de Doully;
    Le Sire de Ollie)
  7 & 8 (Raoul d'Ouilli;
    Robert d'Ouilli)
  Robertus de Oilgi 1086 TC
  Wido de Oilgi 1086 TC
  Radulfus de Oilgi 1086 ST
  Robertus de Oilgi/Olgi
    1086 ST
  Cleveland I 328-331
  (=D'Oyley)
  see also DUILBY
DOYNELL 5 (Doynell)
DRAGANS
  2 (Dragans)
DREUX
  8 (Amauri de Dreux;
    Herman le Dreux)
DRIENCORT
  4 (Sire de Driencort)
  7 (Le Sire de Driencourt)
DRUELL
  1 & 2 & 3 (Druell)
  5 (Druel)
  Amelricus de Dreuues 1086 TC
  Herman de Dreuues 1086 TC
  Cleveland I 293-294

  (=Ruelles)
DRURY
  1 (Drury)
  3 (Diury)
  Cleveland I 345-349
DUGLOSSE
  6 (Le sire Duglosse)
DUILBY see DOYLY
DULEE see DOYLY
DUMARD
  Loyd 38
DUMART see DUMARD
DUMMER
  2 (Dummer)
DUN
  Loyd 38
DUNCHAMPE
  1 (Dunchampe)
  Cleveland I 351-352
DUNSTANVILLE
  Loyd 38-39
DUNSTERUILE
  1 (Dunsteruile)
  Cleveland I 350-351
DURANGE
  1 (Durange)
  Cleveland I 333-334
  (=d'Orenge)
DURANT
  1 & 3 (Durant)
  5 (Duraunt)
  Cleveland I 345
DURAUNT see DURANT
DURVILLE
  8 (Guillaume de Durville)
DUYLLY see DOYLY
DWAI see DOWAI
DYVEYN
  2 (Dyveyn)
EBROIS
  Rogerus de Ebrois 1086 ST
ECALLES see CHALLEYS
ECOUIS see ESCOISECOULAND
  8 (Ecouland)
EINCURIA see AINCOURT
ENGAGNE see ENGAINE
ENGAINE
  1 (Engaine)
  3 (Engayne)
  8 (Richard Engagne)
  Ricardus de Ingania 1086 TC
  Willelmus Ingania 1086 TC
  Cleveland II 9-11
ENISANT
  Enisant 1086 ST
ENVERMOU

Loyd 39
EPINAY see ESPINE
ERARD
    7 (Etienne Erard)
ERCHEMBALD, son of Erchembald the Vicomte; a charter of the Abbey of the Holy Trinity of Rouen, dated within the limits Feb- Dec 1067, records that the monks have redeemed a moiety of the chapel of Holy Trinity by giving six pounds to Erchembald, son of Erchembald the Vicomte, setting out overseas, and twelve pounds to Hugh de Ivry the Butler, who held it on mortgage from the said Erchembald; William, King of the English and Duke of the Normans, and his nobles assenting. It is possible that Erchembald's journey overseas had taken place in the Duke's Army in the previous year, but it is perhaps more likely that the transaction took place when the Conqueror was about to revisit England in December 1067 and that the charter refers to Erchembalds coming voyage in his company.
ESCALERS see CHALLEYS
ESCALLES see CHALLEYS
ESCHETOT
    Loyd 39
ESCOIS
    8 (Guillaume d'Ecouis)
    Willielmus de Scohies
        1086 TC
    Loyd 39-40
ESCRIOLS see CRUEL
ESKETOT see ESCHETOT
ESMALEVILLA
    Willielmus de Malauill
        1086 ST
    Loyd 40
ESPAGNE see HISPANIA
ESPEC
    8 (Guillaume Espec)
ESPINE
    4 (Cil d'Espine)
    7 (Le Sire d'Epinay)
ESTOTEVIL(L)E see ESTOUTEVILLE
ESTOURMI see ESTURMY
ESTOUTEVILLE
    1 (Estuteuile)
    2 (Stotevyle)
    3 (Estutauille)
    4 (Sire d'Estotevile)
    5 (Estoteville)
    7 (Robert d'Estouteville)
    Cleveland II 5-9
    Loyd 40
ESTRANGE
    1 (Estrange)
    3 (Estrange; Lestrange)

    5 (Estraunge)
    Cleveland II 1-5
ESTRE
    Loyd 40
ESTRIELS see CRUEL
ESTURMY
    1 & 3 (Esturney)
    5 (Esturmy)
    7 & 8 (Raoul L'Estourmi;
        Richard L'Estourmi)
    Cleveland II 15-17
ESTUTAUILLE see ESTOUTEVILLE
ESTUTEUILE see ESTOUTEVILLE
EU
    4 (Quens d'Ou)
    7 (Robert Comte d'Eu)
    8 (Guillaume d'Eu;
        Osberne d'Eu;
        Robert, comte d'Eu)
    Osbernus de Ow 1086 ST
    Willelmus de Ow 1086 TC & ST
    Loyd 40
EUDO DAPIFER
    Eudo Dapifer 1086 TC
    Eudo filius Huberti 1086 TC
    Loyd 40
EUERS
    3 (Euers)
    Cleveland III 296
EUSTACY
    5 (Eustacy)
    Cleveland III 372
EVREUX
    7 & 8 (Guillaume, Comte d'Evreux;
        Roger d'Evreux)
    Loyd 41
William of Evreux, mentioned by William of Poitiers and Orderic, was undoubtedly at the Battle. He was grandson ofRobert, Count of Evreux and Archbishop of Rouen, son of Richard I of Normandy. William's sister and heiress carried the comte of Evreux into the family of Montfort-Amaury, from which sprang Simon de Montfort.
EVYLE
    2 (Evyle)
FACONBRIGE see FACUNBERGE
FACUNBERGE
    1 (Facunberge)
    3 (Faconbrige)
    Cleveland II 44-47
FAFITON
    Robertus Fafiton 1086 TC
FALAISE see FALEISE
FALEISE
    8 (Guillaume de Falaise)

47

Willelmus de Faleise 1086 TC
FANECOURT see FAUECOURT
FANENCORT see FAUECOURT
FANUCURT see FAUECOURT
FAUECOURT
  1 (Fauecourt)
  3 (Fanecourt)
  Cleveland II 24-25
  Loyd 41 (Fanecurt)
  see also PENECORD
    & VENICORDE
FAUNUILE see FLAMUILE
FAVARCHES
  Loyd 41
FECAMP see FESCAMP
FELEBERT
  5 (Felebert)
FELGERES
  4 (Cil de Felgieres)
  Radulfus de Felgeres 1086 TC
  Ralph de Felgeres 1086 ST
  Willelmus de Felgeres
    1086 TC
FELGIERES see FELGERES
FENES
  5 (Fenes)
FENIERS
  5 (Feniers)
FERERERS see FERRERS
FERERS see FERRERS
FERGANT/FERGANZ see BRITTANY
FERITATE
  Loyd 41-42
FERMBAUD
  5 (Fermbaud)
FERNZ
  2 (Fernz)
FERRERERS see FERRERS
FERRERS 1 (Ferrers; Ferrerers)
  2 (Ferers)
  4 (Sire de Ferrieres)
  5 (Fererers)
  6 (Henry sire de Ferrers)
  7 (Guillaume de Ferrieres;
    Henri de Ferrieres)
  8 (Henri de Ferrieres)
  Henricus de Ferieres/
    Ferreires/Ferrieres/
    Ferrariis 1086 TC
  Hermerus de Ferreris 1086 TC
  Cleveland II 25-30
  Loyd 42
FERRIERES see FERRERS
FERTE
  4 (Sire de la Ferte)
  7 (Mathieu de la Ferte-Mace)

FESCAMP
  1 (Fleschampe)
  6 (Sire de Fescamp)
  8 (Guillaume de Fecamp)
  Cleveland II 73-74
FEUGERES
  6 (Le sire de Feugiers)
  7 (Raoul de Fougeres)
  8 (Guillaume de Fougeres;
    Raoul de Fougeres)
  Loyd 42-43
FEUGIERS see FEUGERES
FIBERD see FILBERD
FICHET
  1 (Fichet)
  5 (Fichent)
  Cleveland II 68-69
FILBERD
  1 (Filberd)
  3 (Fiberd)
  Cleveland II 23-24
  (= St Philibert)
FILIOLL
  1 & 3 (Filioll)
  5 (Filiol)
  Cleveland II 51-53
FILIOT
  1 (Filiot)
  Cleveland II 30-32 (=Foliot)
FINERE
  1 (Finere)
  3 (Finer)
  Cleveland II 58-60
  (=Finemore)
FitzALAYNE see FitzALLEN
FitzALEYN(E) see FitzALLEN
FitzALLEN
  1 (FitzAleyn)
  3 (FitzAlyne)
  5 (FitzAlayne; FitzAleyne)
FitzALYNE see FitzALLEN
FitzARVIZ
  5 (FitzArviz)
  Cleveland III 372
FitzAUGER
  1 (FitzAuger)
  Cleveland II 41
FitzBERTRAN
  4 (De Peleit le fitz Bertran)
FitzBRIAN
  5 (FitzBrian)
FitzBROWNE
  1 & 3 (FitzBrowne)
  Cleveland I 114-120
FitzERNEIS
  4 (Robert filz Erneis)

6 (Robert le fits Herneys,
   duke Dorlians)
7 (Robert Fitz-Erneis)
Wace asserts that Robert fitz Erneis fought and died at the Battle. Confirmation may be found in a charter of the Abbey of Fontenay issued by a descendant of Robert in 1217 which says that he was killed in England in the time of the Conqueror. Proof is lacking and G.H. White produces evidence to show that he may still have been alive in 1091.

FitzEUSTACE
   1 (FitzEustach)
   5 (FitzEustace)
   Cleveland II 58
FitzEUSTACH see FitzEUSTACE
FitzFITZ
   1 (FitzFitz)
   Cleveland II 69-73
FitzFLAALD
   7 (Alain FitzFlaald)
FitzFOUK
   1 (FitzFouk)
   Cleveland II 51
FitzGEFFREY
   1 (FitzGeffrey)
   Cleveland II 60-61
FitzGEROUD
   8 (Robert fils de Geroud)
FitzHENRIE see FitzHENRY
FitzHENRY
   1 (FitzHenrie)
   5 (FitzHenry)
   Cleveland II 54
FitzHERBERT
   1 (FitzHerbert)
   3 (FitzsHerbert)
   Cleveland II 61-68
FitzHUGH 1 & 3 & 5 (FitzHugh)
   Cleveland II 53-54
FitzIOHN see FitzJOHN
FitzJOHN
   1 & 3 (FitzIohn)
   Cleveland II 73
FitzLAURENCE
   1 (FitzLaurence)
   Cleveland II 58
Fiz de LOU
   2 (Fiz de Lou)
FitzMARMADUKE
   1 & 5 (FitzMarmaduke)
   3 (FitzMarmadux)
   Cleveland II 18-19
FitzMARMADUX see FitzMARMADUKE
FitzMORICE
   1 & 3 & 5 (FitzMorice)
   Cleveland II 53

FitzNELE
   5 (FitzNeel)
   Cleveland III 372-373
FitzOSBERN
   4 (Guillaume fils Osber
      de Bretuil)
   6 (Guilliam Fitz Osberne)
   7 (Guillaume FitzOsberne)
   8 (Guillaume fils d'Osberne)
   Loyd 42
   William FitzOsbern, afterwards 1st Earl of Hereford, mentioned by William of Poitiers and Orderic, was undoubtedly at the Battle. He was the son of Osbern de Crepon and grandson of Herfast the Dane, brother of the Duchess Gunnor. His elder son, William de Breteuil, died without legitimate issue, but the second son Roger, 2nd Earl of Hereford, who lost his Earldom and estates for treason in 1074, left two sons who were probably legitimate, and one of whom was progenitor of the baronial family of Ballon, which seems to have petered out about the beginning of the fourteenth century. See also BRETEVILE.
FitzOTES
   1 (FitzOtes)
   Cleveland II 33-40
FitzPAIN(E) see FitzPAYNE
FitzPAYNE
   1 (FitzPain)
   3 (FitzPaine)
   5 (FitzPayne)
   Cleveland II 41
FitzPERES
   1 (FitzPeres)
   5 (FitzPeris)
   Cleveland II 68
FitzPERIS see FitzPERES
FitzPHILIP
   1 & 3 & 5 (FitzPhilip)
   Cleveland II 30
FitzRAINOLD see FitzRAYNALD
FitzRALPH
   1 (FitzRauff)
   3 (FitzRaulfe)
   5 (FitzRalph; FitzRauf)
   Cleveland II 42
FitzRAUF(F) see FitzRALPH
FitzRAULFE see FitzRALPH
FitzRAYNALD
   1 (FitzRainold)
   5 (FitzRaynald)
   Cleveland II 55-57
FitzREWES
   1 (FitzRewes)
   4 (Tostein fitz Rou II Blanc)

49

7 (Toustain Fitz-Rou)
8 (Turstain fils de Rou)
Cleveland II 69 (=FitzRou)
Turstin FitzRou, mentioned by Orderic, was undoubtedly at the Battle, bearing the ducal banner. Subsequently he is found holding land on the Welsh Marches. Nothing is known of his father, and he seems to have left no issue.
FitzROAND see FitzROHAUT
FitzROBERT
  1 & 3 (FitzRobert)
  5 (twice; FitzRobert)
  Cleveland II 60
FitzROGER
  1 & 3 & 5 (FitzRoger)
  Cleveland II 60
FitzROHAUT
  1 (FitzRoand)
  5 (FitzRohaut)
  Cleveland II 40-41
FitzROU see FitzREWES
FitzSIMON
  1 & 5 (FitzSimon)
  Cleveland II 51
FitzTHOMAS
  1 & 3 & 5 (FitzThomas)
  Cleveland II 53
Fitz d'UNSPAC
  8 (Toustain fils d'Unspac)
FitzURSE
  2 (Fizowres)
  3 (FitzVrcy)
  Cleveland III 296-299
FitzVRCY see FitzURSE
FitzWALTER
  1 & 3 (FitzWater)
  5 (FitzWalter)
  Cleveland II 18
FitzWAREN see FitzWARREN
FitzWARIN see FitzWARREN
FitzWARREN
  1 (FitzWaren)
  3 (FitzWarren)
  5 (Fitzwarin)
  Cleveland II 54-55
FitzWATER see FitzWALTER
FitzWILLIAM
  1 & 3 & 5 (FitzWilliam)
  Cleveland II 40
FIZ de LOU
  2 (Fiz de Lou)
FIZOWRES see FitzURSE
FLAMAND
  7 (Gautier Le Flamand)
  8 (Baudoin Le Flamand; Eude Le Flamand; Gerboud Le Flamand;

Guinemard Le Flamand; Hugue Le Flamand; Josce Le Flamand)
FLAMBARD see FLANBARD
FLAMME
  Rannulfus Flamme 1086 TC
FLAMUILE
  1 (Flamuile)
  3 (Faunuile)
  Cleveland II 57-58
FLANBARD or FLANBART
  8 (Renouf Flambard)
  Rannulfus Flanbard 1086 TC
  Rannulfus Flanbart 1086 TC
FLESCHAMPE see FESCAMP
FLEUEZ
  1 (Fleuez)
  Cleveland II 19-23
  (=Fiennes)
FLIOT
  5 (Fliot)
FLOC
  Loyd 43
FOKE see FOUKE
FOLET see FOLIOT
FOLEVILLE see FOLUILLE
FOLIE
  Loyd 43
FOLIOT
  8 (Guillaume Folet)
  Loyd 43-44
FOLUILLE
  1 (Foluille)
  3 (Foluile)
  5 (Foleville)
  Cleveland II 17-18
FONTENEY
  4 (Le sire de Fontenai)
  6 (Le sire Fonteney)
  8 (Etienne de Fontenai)
  Loyd 44 (Fontenay)
  see also MARMION
FORET
  8 (Guillaume de La Foret)
FORMAY
  1 & 3 (Formay)
  Cleveland II 58
FORMIBAUD
  1 (Formibaud)
  3 (Formiband)
  Cleveland II 58
FORNEUS see FURNIUAUS
FORNYVAUS see FURNIUAUS
FORT
  1 (Fort)
  Cleveland II 47-48
FOSSARD/FOSSART

8 (Neel Fossard)
Nigellus Fossard 1086 TC
Nigellus Fossart 1086 TC
FOUGERES see FEUGERES
FOUKE
1 (Fouke)
3 (Foke)
Cleveland II 42-43
FOURNEAUX see FURNIUAUS
FOURNEUX see FURNIUAUS
FOURNIVAUS see FURNIUAUS
FOVECOURT
5 (Fovecourt)
FRAELVILLA
Loyd 44
FRAMAN
8 (Raoul Framan)
FREANUILE
6 (Le sire de Freanuile)
FRESLE
8 (Richard Fresle)
FRESNE
Loyd 44
FRESSEL
5 (Fressel)
FRESSENVILLE
Loyd 44
FREUIL
1 (Freuil)
3 (Freuile)
5 (Fryville)
Cleveland II 43-44
FREYN
2 (Freyn)
FRIARDEL
Loyd 44FRIBOIS
7 (Le Sire de Fribois)
8 (De Fribois)
FRISELL
1 (Frisell)
3 (Frissell)
Cleveland II 48-51 (=Fraser)
FRISON see FRISOUND
FRISOUND
1 (Frisound)
3 (Frison)
5 (Frisoun)
Cleveland II 58
FROISSART
Willielmus Froissart 1086 ST
FROMENT
8 (Robert Froment)
FRONT DE BOEF
1 (Front de Boef)
FRYVILLE see FREUIL
FULGERIIS see FEUGERES

FUNTENAY see FONTENAY
FURNIUAUS
1 (Furniuaus; Furniueus)
2 (Fornyvaus; Forneus)
5 (Fourneux; Fournivaus)
7 (Eudes de Fourneaux)
8 (Eude de Fourneaux)
Cleveland II 32-33
(=Furneaux)
FURNIUALE
1 (Furniuale)
3 (Furniuall)
Cleveland II 60
FYENS
2 (Fyens)
GACE
6 (Le Sire de Gace)
GACY
6 (le sire de Gacy)
GADOMO see CADOMO
GAEL
4 (Raol de Gael)
6 (Raoul de Gael)
7 & 8 (Raoul de Gael)
GALOFER see GOLOFRE
GAMAGES
1 & 3 (Gamages)
Cleveland II 128-129
Loyd 45
GAND see GAUNT
GANT see GAUNT
GAREN(N)ES see WARENNE
GARGRAUE
3 (Gargraue)
Cleveland III 299
GARRE
5 (Garre)GASCOYNE
3 (Gascoyne)
Cleveland III 303-307
GASIE
4 (Cil de Gasie)
GAUGY
1 & 5 (Gaugy)
Cleveland II 84-86 (=Gage)
GAUNSON
1 (Gaunson)
Cleveland II 97
(=Graunson, q.v.)
GAUNT
3 & 5 (Gaunt)
7 & 8 (Gilbert de Gand)
Gislebertus de Gand/Gant
1086 TC
Cleveland III 307-311
(=Gand/Gant)
GAY see IAY

51

GENEVILE
 2 (Geynevyle)
 5 (Genevile)
GEORGES see GORGES
GERDOUN
 5 (Gerdoun)
GERNOUN
 1 (Gernoun)
 7 (Robert Guernon, Sire de
 Montfiquet)
 8 (Robert Guernon;
 Toustain de Guernon)
 Robertus Gernon 1086 ST
 Robertus Greno
 seu Grenon 1086 TC
 Cleveland II 103-108
GEROUN
 5 (Geroun)
 Cleveland III 373-374
GERY see GURRY
GEYNEVYLE see GENEVILE
GIBARD
 8 (Gilbert Gibard)
GIFFARD
 1 (Giffard)
 2 (Gyffard)
 4 (Galtier Giffart)
 5 (Gifard)
 **7 (Berenger Giffard; Osberne
 Giffard; Gautier Giffard,
 Comte de Longueville)**
 **8 (Berenger Giffard; Fouke
 Giffard; Osberne Giffard)**
 Berenger Gifard 1086 TC
 Osbernus Gifard 1086 TC
 **Walterus Gifard/
 Gifart 1086 TC Cleveland II 120-127**
 Loyd 45
**Walter Giffard, Lord of Longueville, mentioned
by William of Poitiers and Orderic, was
undoubtedly at the Battle. He was son of Osbern
de Bolebec by a sister of Gunnor, Duchess of
Normandy. His line ended with his grandson,
Walter Giffard, 2nd Earl of Buckingham.**
GIFFART see GIFFARD
GILEBOF
 5 (Gilebof)
GINES
 1 (Gines)
 Cleveland II 110-111
GIRARD
 8 (Girard)
GIRON
 Loyd 45
GIRUNDE see GIRON
GISORS

Loyd 45-46
GLANCOURT
 5 (Glancourt)
 8 (Gautier de Grancourt)
 Walterus de Grantcurt
 1086 ST
 Cleveland III 374-375
 Loyd 47 (Grandcourt)
 Loyd 48 (Grincurt)
GLANVILLE
 3 (Glanuile)
 7 (Le Sire de Glanville)
 7 (Robert de Glanville)
 Ro(t)bertus de Glanvill/
 Glanvilla 1086 ST
 Cleveland III 299-303
 Loyd 46
GLATEUILE
 1 (Glateuile)
 Cleveland II 120
 (=Granteville)
GLAPION
 Loyd 46-47
GLOS see GLOZ
GLOZ
 4 (Cil de Gloz)
 7 (Le Sire de Glos)
GOBAND
 1 (Goband)
 5 (Gobaude)
 Cleveland II 86 (=Gobaud)
GOBAUDE see GOBAND
GOBION
 1 (Gobion)
 5 (Gubion)
 Cleveland II 98GOLOFRE
 1 (Golofre)
 3 (Golofer)
 5 (Galofer)
 8 (Guillaume Goulaffre)
 Willielmus Gulaffra 1086 ST
 Willielmus Gulafra 1086 ST
 Cleveland II 97-98
 (=Golafre)
GOMER
 2 (Gomer)
GONYS
 6 (Le sire de Gonys)
GORBET see CORBET
GORGEISE
 5 (Gorgeise)
GORGES
 1 (Georges)
 2 (Gorges)
 Cleveland II 81-82
GORNAI see GOURNAY

GORNAY see GOURNAY
GOUER see GOWER
GOUERGES
  1 (Couerges)
  7 (Geoffroi de la Guierche)
  8 (Geoffroi de La Guierche)
  Cleveland II 127-128
  (=Guierche)
GOULAFFRE see GOLOFRE
GOURNAY
  1 (Gurnay; Gurney)
  2 (Gornay)
  4 (Hue de Gornai)
  5 (Gurnay)
  6 (Le Conte Hue de Gournay;
    Hue de Gournay sire
    le de Bray)
  7 (Hugue de Gournay; Hugue de
    Gournay, Le Jeune)
  8 (Hugue de Gournai;
    Neel de Gournai)
  Hugo de Gurnai 1086 TC
  Cleveland II 74-77
  Loyd 47
GOUVIX see GOVIZ
GOVIZ
  4 (Cil de Goviz)
  7 (Guillaume de Gouvix)
GOWER
  1 & 5 (Gower)
  3 (Gouer)
  Cleveland II 82-84
GRACY
  1 & 3 (Gracy)
  Cleveland II 80-81
GRAI see GRAY
GRAINVILLE see GRENVILLE
GRAMMORI
  1 (Grammori)
  Cleveland II 102-103
GRANCOURT see GLANCOURT
GRANCURT see GLANCOURT
GRANDCOURT see GLANCOURT
GRANDMESNIL see GRENTEMAISNIL
GRANTCURT see GLANCOURT
GRAUNDYN see GRENDON
GRAUNGERS
  2 (Graungers)
GRAUNS
  3 (Grauns)
GRAUNSON
  1 & 3 (Graunson)
  5 (twice; Graunson)
  Cleveland II 78-80 (=Grandison)
  see also GAUNSON
GRAUNT

1 (Graunt)
  Cleveland II 98-100
GRAY
  1 & 2 & 3 & 5 (Gray)
  8 (Anquetil de Grai)
  Anchitillus de Grai 1086 ST
  Cleveland II 87-97
GREILE
  1 (Greile)
  5 (Greilly)
  Cleveland II 100
GREILLY see GREILE
GREINVILLE see GRENVILLE
GRENDON
  1 (Grendon)
  5 (Graundyn)
  Cleveland II 108-109
GRENEUILE
  1 (Greneuile)
  Cleveland II 112-120
GRENSY
  1 (Grensy)
GRENTEMAISNIL
  4 (Un vassal de Grentemesnil)
  7 & 8 (Hugue de Grentemesnil)
  Hugo de Grentemaisnil
    1086 TC
  Loyd 47
Hugh de Grandmesnil, mentioned by William of
Poitiers and Orderic, was undoubtedly at the
Battle. He was the son of Robert de
Grandmesnil, and received great estates in
England, which his fourth son Ives mortgaged
and lost to Robert, Count of Meulan and Earl of
Leicester. The eldest son Robert succeeded to the
Norman honour of Grandmesnil, which his
grand-daughter and heiress eventually carried to
Robert, 3rd Earl of Leicester.
GRENTEMESNIL see GRENTEMAISNIL
GRENTEVILLE
  8 (Turold de Grenteville)
GRENVILLE
  Loyd 47-48
GRESLET
  8 (Aubert Greslet)
  Albertus Greslet 1086 ST
GRESSY
  1 (Gressy)
  Cleveland II 78
GRETEVILLA
  Turaldus de Greteuilla
    1086 TC
GREUET
  1 (Greuet)
  Cleveland II 100-101
  (=Gemet)

53

GREVEQUER see CREVEQUER
GREVYLE see GRIUIL
GREYLE
  2 (Greyle)
GRIKETOT
  5 (Griketot)
  see also CRIKETOT
GRIMSUILLE
  6 (Le sire de Grimsuille)
GRINCURT see GLANCOURT
GRINNOSAVILLA
  Loyd 48
GRIUIL
  1 (Griuil)
  2 (Grevyle)
  5 (Gruyele)
  Cleveland II 111-112
  (=Greville)
GROSVENOR see VENOURE
GRUYELE see GRIUIL
GRYMWARD
  5 (Grymward)
GUBION
  5 (Gubion)
GUERNON see GERNOUN
GUERRIS see GWERES
GUERY see GURRY
GUIERCHE see GOUERGES
GULAFRA see GOLOFRE
GURDON
  1 & 3 (Gurdon)
  Cleveland II 109-110
GURLEY
  1 (Gurley)
  3 (Gurly)
  Cleveland II 102
GURNAY see GOURNAY
GURNEY see GOURNAY
GURRY
  1 (Gurry)
  Cleveland II 101-102
  (=Guery or Gery)
GWERES
  Loyd 48-49
GYFFARD see GIFFARD
HACHET see HAKETT
HAGA see HAIG
HAIA see DELAHAY
HAIE see DELAHAY
HAIG
  Loyd 49-50
HAKETT
  1 (Hakett)
  3 (Hecket)
  7 & 8 (Gautier Hachet)
  Cleveland II 156-158

HALUILE
  Radulfus de Haluile 1086 TC
HAMELIN
  1 (Hamelin)
  3 (Hamelyn)
  5 (Hameline)
  Hamelin 1086 ST
  Hamelinus 1086 TC
  Cleveland II 152-154
HAMO DAPIFER
  Loyd 50
HAMOUND
  1 & 3 (Hamound)
  Cleveland II 158
HANLAY see HAULAY
HANSARD
  1 & 2 & 5 (Haunsard)
  3 (Hansard)
  Cleveland II 130-131
HARCORD see HARECOURT
HARCOURT see HARECOURT
HARDELL
  1 (Hardell)
  3 (Hardel)
  Cleveland II 156
HARECORD see HARECOURT
HARECOURT
  1 (Harecourt & Harcord)
  2 & 5 (Harecourt)
  3 (Harecord)
  4 (Sire de Herecort)
  6 (Le sire de Harecourt)
  7 (Robert de Harcourt;
    Errand de Harcourt)
  8 (Robert de Harcourt)
  Cleveland II 148-151
  Loyd 51 (Harcourt)
HAREVILLE
  5 (Hareville)HAREWELL
  1 & 3 (Harewell)
  Cleveland II 154-156
HASTINGS
  1 & 3 & 5 (Hastings)
  2 (Hastyng)
  Rad. de Hastings 1086 ST
  Robertus de Hastinges
    1086 ST
  Cleveland II 131-137
HASTYNG see HASTINGS
HAULAY
  1 (Hanlay)
  3 (Haulay)
  5 (Haulley)
  Cleveland II 137 (=Hauley)
HAULLEY see HAULAY
HAUNSARD see HANSARD

HAUNTENY see HAUTEYN
HAURELL
  1 (Haurell)
  Cleveland II 137-138
  (=Harel)
HAUSTLAYNG
  2 (Haustlayng)
HAUTAIN see HAUTEYN
HAUTEIN see HAUTEYN
HAUTEVILE
  2 (Hautevyle)
  5 (Hauville)
  8 (Raoul de Hauville)
  Cleveland III 375-377
HAUTEYN
  1 (Haunteny)
  2 (Hauteyn)
  5 (Hautein)
  Cleveland II 129-130
HAUVILLE see HAUTEVILE
HAY see DELAHAY
HAYE see DELAHAY
HAYWARD
  5 (Hayward)
  Cleveland III 377-378
HECKET see HAKETT
HELION
  2 (Holyon)
  8 (Herve d'Helion)
  Loyd 51
HENOUR see HENOURE
HENOURE
  1 (Henoure)
  5 (Henour)
  Cleveland II 151
HERCY
  1 (Hercy)
  5 (Hercy; Heryce)
  7 (Hugue d'Hericy)
  8 (D'Hericy)
  Cleveland II 141-142
HERECORT see HARECOURT
HERICY see HERCY
HERION see HERIOUN
HERIOUN
  1 (Herioun)
  5 (Heroun)
  Tehellus de Herion 1086 TC
  Tihellus de Herion 1086 ST
  Cleveland II 142-144
  (=Heron)
HERNE
  1 & 3 (Herne)
  Cleveland II 144-148
  (=Herice)
HERON see HERIOUN

HEROUN see HERIOUN
HERYCE see HERCY
HESDIN
  8 (Arnoul de Hesdin)
  Ernulfus de Hesding 1086 TC
  Loyd 51
HEUSE see HEWSE and HUSEE
HEWSE
  1 (Dehense)
  3 (de Hewse)
  8 (Gautier Heuse)
  see also HUSEE
HILL see DELAHILL
HISPANIA
  8 (Auvrai d'Espagne;
    Herve d'Espagne)
  Aluredus Hispaniensis
    seu de Ispania 1086 TC
  Loyd 51-52
HISPANIENSIS see HISPANIA
HODENC
  8 (Hugue de Hodenc)
HOLYON see HELION
HOMME
  6 (Le sire de Homme)
le HOMMET
  Loyd 52
HOSED
  Willelmus Hosed 1086 TC
  Walterus Hosed 1086 ST
HOTO
  8 (Hugue de Hoto)
  see also HOUDETOT
HOUDETOT
  7 (Hugue d'Houdetot)
  8 (D'Houdetot)
  see also HOTO
HOUELL
  1 (Houell)
  Cleveland II 151-152
  (=Hovel)HOWARDE
  5 (Howarde)
  Cleveland III 378-379
HOWELL
  5 (Howell)
HULDBYNSE
  2 (Huldbynse)
HURELL
  5 (Hurell)
HUSAY see HUSEE
de la HUSE
  5 (de la Huse)
HUSEE
  1 & 5 (Husee)
  2 (Husay & Husee)
  3 (Husie)

Cleveland II 138-141
(=Hussey)
see also de HEWSE
HUSIE see HUSEE
HUSSEY see HUSEE
HYLDEBROND
2 (Hyldebrond)
HYNOYS
2 (Hynoys)
IANUILE
1 & 3 (Ianuile)
Cleveland II 161-163
(=Joinville
and Geneville)
IARDEN
1 & 3 (Iarden)
5 (Jardin)
Cleveland II 159
(=Garden)
IASPERUILE
1 (Iasperuile)
3 (Iasparuile)
Cleveland II 163
(=Jarpenville)
IAY
1 & 3 (Iay)
5 (Jay)
Cleveland II 159-160
(=Gay)
IENIELS
1 (Ieniels)
Cleveland II 160-161
(=Juel/Jewell)
IERCONUISE
1 (Ierconuise)
Cleveland II 161
(=Jerconville)
ILE see ISLE
INCOURT
8 (Gautier d'Incourt)
INGANIA
Ricardus de Ingania 1086 TC
Willielmus Inganie 1086 ST
INSULA see ISLE
IORT
4 (Cil de Jort)
6 (Le sire de Iort)
7 (Le Sire de Jort)
ISLE
2 (Yle)
3 (de Liele;
Lislay vel Liele)
5 (de l'Isle)
8 (Honfroi del'Ile;
Raoul de l'Ile)
Hunfridus de Insula 1086 TC

Radulfus de Insula 1086 TC
Cleveland III 312-324
IVERI
7 (Jean d'Ivri)
8 (Archard d'Ivri; Hugue d'Ivri;
Roger d'Ivri)
Hugo & Rogerus de Iveri
1086 TC
Acardus de Iuri 1086 ST
Rogerus de Ivri/Iurei/Juri
1086 ST
Loyd 52 (Ivry)
IVRI see IVERI
IVRY see IVERI
JARDIN see IARDEN
JARPENVILLE see IASPERUILE
JAY see IAY
JERCONVILLE see IERCONUISE
JEWELL see IENIELS
JORT see IORT
JORY see ST. JORY
JUEL see IENIELS
JURI see IVERI
KAILLI see CAILLI
KANCEIS
5 (Kanceis)
KANCEY
1 (Kancey)
Cleveland II 176 (=Chancy)
KANTILUPO see CANTELOU
KARRE
1 & 3 (Karre)
Cleveland II 164-168 (=Ker)
KARRON see KARROWE
KARROWE
1 (Karrowe)
3 (Karron)
Cleveland II 168-169
(=Carew)
KAUNT
1 (Kaunt)
Cleveland II 163
KENELRE
1 (Kenelre)
5 (Kevelers)
Cleveland II 176
(=Kevelers=Chivaler)
KER see KARRE
KEVELERS see KENELRE
KEYNES see CAHAGNES
KIMARONNE
1 (Kimaronne)
Cleveland II 175
KIRIELL see CRUEL
KNEVYLE see NEVILLE
KOINE

1 (Koine)
Cleveland II 169-175
(=Cahaignes=Cheney)
KYMARAYS
5 (Kymarays)
KYRIEL see CRUEL
KYRIELL see CRUEL
LACELLES see LASCALES
LACEY see LACY
LACY
1 (Lacy; twice)
2 (Lacy)
4 (Chevalier de Lacie;
Cil de Lacie)
5 (Lascy)
6 (Le sire de Lacy)
7 (Gautier de Lacy;
Ibert de Lacy)
8 (Gautier de Laci; Hugue de Laci;
Ibert de Laci; Roger de Laci)
Ilbertus de Laci 1086 TC/ST
Rogerus de Laci 1086 TC/ST
Walterus de Laci 1086 ST
Cleveland II 176-181
Loyd 53 (Lascy)
LAIGLE
4 (Engerran de Laigle)
6 (Enguemount de Laigle)
7 & 8 (Engenoulf de l'Aigle)
Loyd 52
Engenulf de Laigle, mentioned by Orderic, was undoubtedly at the Battle. He was son of Foubert de Beine, who built the castle of Laigle — so called because the workmen found an eagle's nest in an oak near by — on the Risle. Engenulf was the only prominent Norman who lost his life in the Battle, being killed in the later stages when the pursuing Norman cavalry fell into the "malefosse". He was succeeded by his son Richer de Laigle (slain in 1084), whose issue held the lordship of Pevensey, hence sometimes known as the Honor of the Eagle. Laigle, or theEagle, was latinized as "de Aquila", and Richer's younger brother was the "Gilbert de Aquila" who will be well known to the readers of Kipling's books, "Puck of Pook's Hill" and "Rewards and Fairies".
de LALAUND see LANDE
LAMBERT
7 (Raoul Lambert)
LA MUILE see LAUMALE
LANDE or LAUNDE
4 (Willame Patric
de la Lande)
5 (De la Laund; De Lalaund)
6 (Guilliam Patris

de la Land)
7 (Guillaume Patry
de la Lande)
Loyd 76 (Patric)
LANDRI
8 (Landri)
LANE
1 (Lane)
3 (Laue)
7 (Hugue L'Asne)
8 (Hugue L'Ane)
Hugo Asne seu Asinus 1086 TC
Hugo Lasne 1086 TC
Cleveland II 220-223
(=L'Asne)
LANFRANC
8 (Lanfranc)
LANGETOT
8 (Raoul de Languetot)
Radulfus de Langetot 1086 ST
Radulfus de Langhetot
1086 ST
Loyd 53
LANGHETOT see LANGETOT
LANGUETOT see LANGETOT
LANVALLEI see de la VALET
LASCALES
1 (Lascales)
3 (Lastels)
5 (Lascels)
7 (Guillaume de Lacelles)
Willielmus de Locels 1086 ST
Cleveland II 208-210
(=Lascelles)
Loyd 55 (Locels)
LASCELS see LASCALES
LASCY see LACY
LASERT
6 (Le sire de Lasert)
LASNE see LANE
LASTELS see LASCALES
LATIMER see LATOMER
LATOMER
1 (Latomer)
3 (Latomere)
5 (Latymer)
Cleveland II 184-187
(=Latimer)
LATYMER see LATOMER
LAUE see LANE
LAUMALE
1 (Laumale)
5 (la Muile)
Cleveland II 218-220
(=Albemarle)
Cleveland III 379

LAUNAY see LUNY
LAUND see LANDE
LAVAL
  7 (Guy de la Val;
    Hamon de la Val)
  Loyd 53
LEDED
  1 (Leded)
  Cleveland II 210-211
  (=Laidet)
LEMARE
  1 & 3 (Lemare)
  Cleveland II 191-196
  (=de la Mare)
LENIAS
  5 (Lenias)
LESCROPE see SCROPE
LESTRANGE see ESTRANGE
LESTRE
  Loyd 53-54
LETRE
  8 (Guillaume de Letre)
LEUEL
  3 (Leuel)
  5 (Levele)
LEUETOT
  1 (Leuetot; Louetot)
  5 (Levecote)
  Cleveland II 196-198
  (=Lovetot)
  Loyd 55-56 (Luvetot)
LEUONY see LOUENY
LEVECOTE see LEUETOT
LEVELE see LEUEL
LEWAWSE
  3 (Lewawse)
  Cleveland III 324-325
LICHARE
  4 (Sire de Litehare)
  6 (Le sire de Lichare)
  7 (Le Sire de Lithaire)
LIELE see ISLE
LIFFORD see OLIFANT
LIMERS   1 & 5 (Limers)
  Cleveland II 21
LIMESI
  1 (Linneby)
  3 (Lindsey)
  5 (Lymesey)
  7 & 8 (Raoul de Limesi)
  Radulfus de Limesi sive
    Limeseio 1086 TC
  Cleveland II 181
  (=Limesey=Lindsay)
  Loyd 54 (Limesi)
de la LIND see DELALINDE

LINDSEY see LIMESI
LINNEBY see LIMESI
LINGIEURE
  Loyd 54
LIOF
  5 (Liof)
  Liofus 1086 TC/ST
  Cleveland III 382
LIONS
  7 (Ingelram de Lions)
LISIEUX
  8 (Roger de Lisieux)
LISLAY see ISLE
LISLE see ISLE
LISORS see LISOURS
LISOURS
  5 (Lisours)
  8 (Fouque de Lisors)
  Fulco de Lusorio 1086 ST
  Fulco de Lusoriis 1086 TC
  Cleveland III 380-382
LITEHARE see LICHARE
LITHAIRE see LICHARE
LITTERILE
  3 (Litterile)
LIVET
  Loyd 55
LOCELS see LASCALES
LOGENTON
  3 (Logenton)
  Cleveland III 311
LOGES
  2 (Loges)
  8 (Biget de Loges)
LOGEUILE see LONGUEVILLE
LOIONS
  1 (Loions)
  Cleveland II 216-218
  (=Lyons)
LONGCHAMP
  1 (Longechampe)
  3 (Lonschampe)
  5 (Longchaumpe)
  Cleveland II 207-208
  Loyd 55
LONGCHAUMPE see LONGCHAMP
LONGECHAMPE see LONGCHAMP
LONGEPAY see LONGESPE
LONGESPAY see LONGESPE
LONGESPE
  1 (Longepay; Longespes)
  2 (Longespay)
  3 (Longspes)
  5 (Longespe)
  Cleveland II 206
LONGESPES see LONGESPE

LONGEUALE see LONGUEVILLE
LONGEVYLE see LONGUEVILLE
LONGNEUILLE see LONGUEVILLE
LONGSPES see LONGESPE
LONGUAILE see LONGUEVILLE
LONGUEVILLE
 1 (Logeuile; Longeuale)
 2 (Longevyle)
 3 (Longuaile)
 5 (Longvil; Longvale)
 6 (Gualtar Guisart,
  Counte de Longneuille)
 Cleveland II 204-206
LONGUS CAMPUS see LONGCHAMP
LONGVALE see LONGUEVILLE
LONGVIL see LONGUEVILLE
LONGVILLERS see LUNGVILERS
LONSCHAMPE see LONGCHAMP
LORANCOURT
 1 (Lorancourt)
 Cleveland II 215-216
 (=Louvencort)
LORING
 1 (Loruge)
 5 (Loring)
 Cleveland II 214-215
 (=Luring)
LORUGE see LORING
LORZ
 8 (Robert de Lorz)
 Robert de Lorz 1086 TC
LOS see LUCY
LOTERELL
 1 (Loterell)
 3 & 5 (Loterel)
 Cleveland II 211-214
 (=Luttrell)
LOU
 2 (Lou)
LOUAN
 1 (Louan)
 Cleveland II 210 (=Lovent)
LOUCELLES
 8 (Guillaume de Loucelles)
LOUEDAY
 1 & 3 (Loueday)
 5 (Loveday)
 Cleveland II 187-188
LOUELL see LOVEL
LOUENY
 1 (Loueny)
 3 (Leuony)
 Cleveland II 176
 (=Louvigny)
LOUERACE
 1 (Louerace)

 Cleveland II 206-207
LOUETOT see LEUETOT
LOUVET see LOVET
LOUVIGNY see LOUENY
LOVEDAY see LOUEDAY
LOVEIN
 2 (Loveyn)
 5 (Lovein; Loveyne)
LOVEL
 1 (Louell)
 2 (Lovell)
 5 (Lovel)
 Louel (miles) 1086 ST
 Cleveland II 188-18
 Loyd 55
LOVERAK
 5 (Loverak)
LOVET
 7 (Guillaume Louvet)
 8 (Guillaume de Louvet)
 Willelmus Lovet 1086 TC
 Willelmus Loveth 1086 TC
LOVEYN see LOVEIN
LOVEYNE see LOVEIN
LOWNAY see LUNY
LOY
 1 & 3 (Loy)
 Cleveland II 215
LUCY
 1 (Lucy & Luse)
 2 & 3 (Lucy)
 5 (Luscy)
 Cleveland II 211 (=Los)
LUNGVILERS
 5 (Lungvilers)
 Cleveland III 379-380
 (=Longvillers)
 Loyd 55 (Longvillers)
LUNY
 1 (Luny)
 5 (Lownay)
 Cleveland II 204 (=Launay)
LURI
 Hugo de Luri 1086 TC
LUSCY see LUCY
LUSE see LUCY
LUSORIIS/LUSORIO see LISOURS
LUVETOT see LEUETOT
LYMESEY see LIMESI
MACI see MASSEY
MAGNAVILLA see MANDEVILLE
MAGNEUILLE see MANDEVILLE
MAGNEVILLA see MANDEVILLE
MAGNEVIL(L)E see MANDEVILLE
MAIELL
 1 (Maiell)

59

3 (Mayel)
Cleveland II 338-339
MAIHERMER
5 (Maihermer)
MAILLARD see MAULARD
MAINARD
1 (twice; Mainard)
3 & 5 (Mainard)
Mainardus homo Rogeri
Pictavensis 1086 ST
Cleveland II 302-304
MAINE
1 (Maine)
Cleveland II 301-302
MAINELL
1 (Mainell)
Cleveland II 305-307
(=Meynell)
MAINERIIS see MEINIERS
MAINGUN
5 (Maingun)
Cleveland III 385
MAINWARING
1 & 3 (Mainwaring)
Cleveland II 332-334
MAITLAND see MONTALENT
MALAON see MELUN
MALAUILL see ESMALEVILLA
MALBEDENG
Willielmus Malbedeng 1086 ST
MALDOIT(H) see MAUDUIT
MALDUIT see MAUDUIT
MALDVITH see MAUDUIT
MALEBERGE
5 (Maleberge)
8 (Auvrai de Merleberge)
Cleveland III 384-385
MALEBOUCH
2 (Malebouch)
5 (Malebuche)
Cleveland III 383
MALEBUCHE see MALEBOUCH
MALEBRANCHE see MALEBRAUNCH
MALEBRAUNCH
1 (Malebraunch)
3 (Malebranche)
Cleveland II 245
MALEBYS
5 (Malebys)
Cleveland III 386-388
MALEHEIRE   1 (Maleheire)
Cleveland II 334
MALEHERBE
1 & 3 (Maleherbe)
2 (Malerbe)
7 (Raoul de Malherbe)

Cleveland II 268-269
MALE KAKE see MELETAK
MALELUSE see MEULES
MALEMAIN see MALEMAINE
MALEMAINE
1 & 3 (Malemaine)
2 (Malemeyn)
5 (Malemayn)
Cleveland II 246-248
MALEMAYN see MALEMAINE
MALEMEYN see MALEMAINE
MALEMIS
1 (Malemis)
Cleveland II 334
MALERBE see MALEHERBE
MALET
1 & 2 & 5 (Malet)
4 (Guillame Mallet)
6 (Guilliam Mallet)
7 (Durand Malet; Gilbert Malet;
Robert Malet;
Guillaume Malet de Graville)
8 (Durand Malet; Gilbert Malet;
Guillaume Malet; Robert
Malet)
Durandus Malet 1086 TC
Robertus Malet 1086 TC/ST
Gislebertus de Malet 1086 ST
Cleveland II 261-264
Loyd 56
William Malet, mentioned by William of Poitiers
and Orderic, was undoubtedly at the Battle. His
parentage is doubtful. His son Robert Malet, who
was Master Chamberlain under Henry I, was
deprived of his estates and banished in or before
1106.
MALEUERE
1 (Maleuere)
5 (Mauliverer)
Cleveland II 312-314
(=Mauleverer)
MALEUILE
1 & 3 (Maleuile)
2 (Malevyle)
5 (Maleville)
8 (Guillaume de Malleville)
Cleveland II 259-261
MALGERI see MEINNIL
MALHERBE see MALEHERBE
MALLARD see MAULARD
MALLET see MALET
MALLEVILLE see MALEUILE
MALLOP
5 (Mallop)
MALLORY
1 (Mallory)

60

3 (Malory)
Cleveland II 280-283
Loyd 56
MALQUENCI
Loyd 56
MALTRAVERS see MONTRAVERS
MALURE
2 (Malure)
MALVESYN
2 (Malvesyn)
MAMINOT
8 (Gilbert Maminot;
Hugue Maminot)
Gislebertus Maminot
1086 TC/ST
Hugo Maminot 1086 ST
Loyd 57
MANDEVILLE
1 (Maundeuile; Manuile)
2 (Maundevyle)
4 (Sire de Magnevile)
5 (Moundevile)
6 (Le Sire de Magneuille;
Le Sire de Margneuille)
7 (Geoffroi de Mandeville)
8 (Geoffroi de Mandeville;
Hugue de Manneville)
Goisfridus de Mannevile
1086 TC
Goisfridus de Manneuile
1086 ST
Hugo de Manneuile 1086 ST
Cleveland II 226-230
Loyd 57-59
see also MONNEVILLE
MANDUT see MAUDUIT
MANDUTE see MAUDUIT
MANERIIS see MEINIERS
MANERS see MINERS
MANFE
1 (Manfe)
Cleveland II 300
MANGISERE
1 (Mangisere)
5 (Mangysir)
Cleveland II 322
MANGNY
6 (Le sire de Mangny)
MANGYSIR see MANGISERE
MANLAY
1 (Manlay; twice)
3 (Manle; Manley)
Cleveland II 330
MANLE see MANLAY
MANLEY see MANLAY
MANNERS see MINERS

MANNEVILLA see MANDEVILLE
MANNEVILLE see MANDEVILLE
MANTEL see MANTELL
MANTELET see MANTELL
MANTELL
1 (Mantelet)
3 (Mantell)
8 (Toustain Mantel)
Turstinus Mantel 1086 TC
Cleveland II 315-316
MANTEUENANT
1 (Manteuenant)
5 (Maucovenant)
Cleveland II 299
(=Mauconvenant)
MANTRAVERS
2 (Mantravers)
MANUILE see MANDEVILLE
MAOUN
5 (Maoun)
MARCEANS
1 (Marceans)
Cleveland II 336-338
(=Monceaux)
see also MONCEAUX
MARCHE
5 (De la Marche)
Cleveland III 370
MARE
1 (Mare; twice)
2 (Mare)
4 (Cil de La Mare)
5 (Marre; De la Mare)
6 (Le sire de la Mare;
Le sire de Marre)
7 & 8 (Guillaume de La Mare;
Hugue de La Mare)
MARESCAL
8 (Geoffroi Le Marechal)
Goisfridus Marescal 1086 TC
Robertus Marescal 1086 TC
Rogerus Marescalchus 1086 TC
Giroldus Mareschalcus 1086 TC
MARESC(H)ALC(H)US see MARESCAL
MARGNEUILLE see MANDEVILLE
MARINNI
Loyd 59
MARIS
2 (Maris)
MARKENFIELD see MERKINGFEL
MARMILON see MARMION
MARMION
1 & 3 (Marmilon)
2 (Marmyoun)
4 (Baron Rogier Marmion)
6 (Rogier Marmion)

7 (Robert Marmion
de Fontenai)
Cleveland II 230-235
Loyd 60
see also FONTENEY
MARMYOUN see MARMION
MARNY
1 & 5 (Marny)
3 (Merny)
Cleveland II 283-284
MARRE see MARE
MARSI
8 (Raoul de Marsi)
MARSTON
Loyd 60
MARTEINE
1 & 3 (Marteine)
5 (Martine)
Cleveland II 256-257
MARTEL
7 & 8 (Geoffroi Martel)
Goisfridus Martel 1086 ST
Loyd 60-61
see also BASKERUILE
MARTIGNY
Loyd 61
MARTINAST see MARTINWAST
MARTINE see MARTEINE
MARTINWAST
1 (Martinast)
Cleveland II 331-332
Loyd 61
MASCY see MASSEY
MASSEY
5 (Mascy)
7 (Hugue de Macey)
8 (Hugue de Maci)
Hugo Maci 1086 ST
Cleveland III 391-394
Loyd 61-62
MATELAY
1 (Matelay)
Cleveland II 334
MATHAN
7 & 8 (De Mathan)
MATUEN
Loyd 62
MAUBANK
2 (Maubank)
8 (Guillaume Maubenc)
MAUBENC see MAUBANK
MAUCHES
5 (Mauches)
Cleveland III 391
MAUCLERK see MAUCLERKE
MAUCLERKE

1 (Mauclerke)
5 (Mauclerk)
Cleveland II 319-320
MAUCOVENANT see MANTEUENANT
MAUCONVENANT see MANTEUENANT
MAUDICT see MAUDUIT
MAUDUIT
1 (Mandut)
2 (Maudut)
3 (Mandute)
5 (Maudict)
8 (Gonfroi Mauduit;
Guillaume Mauduit)
Gunfridus Maldoith 1086 TC
Willelmus Maldvith 1086 TC
Willielmus Maldoit 1086 ST
Cleveland II 314-315
Loyd 62
MAUFE
5 (Maufe)
Cleveland II 300
see also MOUNFEY
MAULARD
1 (Maulard)
Cleveland II 330
(=Maillard or Mallard)
MAULAY see MAULE
MAULE
1 (Maule)
3 & 5 (Mauley)
Cleveland II 245 (Maulay)
and II 295-296 (Maule)
MAULEVERER see MALEUERE
MAULEY see MAULE
MAULIVERER see MALEUERE
MAULOVEL
5 (Maulovel)
MAUMASIN
1 (Maumasin)
5 (Mauveysin)
Cleveland II 322-323
(=Mavesyn)
MAUNCEL
5 (Mauncel)
Cleveland III 394-395
MAUNCHENELL
1 (Maunchenell)
Cleveland II 320
(=Montchevrel)
MAUNDEUILE see MANDEVILLE
MAUNEVILE see MANDEVILLE
MAUNYS
5 (Maunys)
Cleveland III 386
MAUREWARDE see MAWREWARD
MAUROUARD see MAWREWARD

62

MAUTALENT see MONTALENT
MAUTRAUERS see MONTRAVERS
MAUVEYSIN see MAUMASIN
MAVESYN see MAUMASIN
MAWREWARD
1 (Mawreward)
5 (Maurewarde)
8 (Geoffroi Maurouard)
Cleveland II 323
MAYEL see MAIELL
MAYENNE
6 (Gieffray sire de Mayenne)
Loyd 62-63
MEANIE
4 (Gifrei de Meanie)
MEDUANA see MAYENNE
MEINIERS
Loyd 63
MEINNIL
Loyd 63
MEINTENORE
1 (Meintenore)
Cleveland II 320
MEISI
Loyd 64
MELETAK
1 (Meletak)
5 (Male Kake)
Cleveland II 320-321
(=Malecake)
MELLER
1 (Meller)
Cleveland II 325-326
MELUN
1 (Melun)
Cleveland II 335-336
(=Malaon)
MEMOROUS
1 (Memorous)
Cleveland II 310
MENERE
1 (Menere)
Cleveland II 330-331
MENEUILE
1 (Meneuile)
5 (Menevile)
Cleveland II 298-299
MENEVILE see MENEUILE
MENPINCOY
1 & 3 (Menpincoy)
5 (Mounpinson)
Cleveland II 300-301
Loyd 69 (Montpincon)
MENYLE
5 (Menyle)
MERI

8 (Richard de Meri)
MERKE
1 & 3 (Merke)
Cleveland II 277-278
& III 370
MERKINGFEL
5 (Merkingfel)
Cleveland III 385-386
(=Markenfield)
MERLAY
5 (Merlay)
Cleveland III 389-390
MERLE
2 (Merle)
7 & 8 (Du Merle)
MERLEBERGE see MALEBERGE
MERNY see MARNY
MESNI-LE-VILLERS see VILERS
MEULAN
8 (Robert, comte de Meulan)
MEULES
1 (Maleluse)
5 (Meulos)
7 (Baudoin de Meules et du Sap)
8 (Baudoin de Meules;
Roger de Meules)
Cleveland II 307-309
MEULLES see MEULES
MEULOS see MEULES
MEYNELL see MAINELL
MILERS see MILLIERES
MILLEVILLE
Loyd 64
MILLIERES
Loyd 64
MINERIIS see MINERS
MINERS
1 (Miners)
3 (Myners)
5 (Maners)
Cleveland II 316-319
(=Manners)
Loyd 64-65
MIRIELL
1 (Miriell)
Cleveland II 245
MOBEC
8 (Hugue de Mobec)
MOELS
Loyd 65
MOHANT
1 (Mohant; Monhaut)
2 (Mohant)
5 (Mohaut)
Cleveland II 223
(=Monhaut or Montalt)

63

MOHAUT see MOHANT
MOHUN
  1 (Mowne & Moine)
  2 & 5 (Mooun)
  4 (Willame de Moion)
  6 (Guilliam Moyon)
  7 & 8 (Guillaume de Moyon)
  Willelmus de Moion
    seu Moiun 1086 TC
  Willielmus Moion 1086 ST
  Cleveland II 223-226 (Mohun)
    and 273-275 (Moine)
  Loyd 66
MOINE see MOHUN
MOION see MOHUN
MOIUN see MOHUN
MOLEBEC
  Hugo de Molebec 1086 TC
  Hugo Molebec 1086 ST
MOLEI
  4 (Sire del viez Molei)
MOLES see MOELS
MOLETON
  2 (Moleton)
MOLINS
  2 (Molyns)
  4 (Dam Willame des Molins)
  6 (Guilliam de Moulinous)
  7 (Guillaume de Moulins,
    S. de Falaise)
MOLYNS see MOLINS
MOLIS see MOELS
MONAY see MOUET
MONBRAI see MOWBRAY
MONCEALS see MONCEAUX
MONCEAUX
  4 (Cil de Monceals)
  5 (Mounceus; Mouncy)
  7 & 8 (Guillaume de Monceaux)
  Cleveland III 390-391
    (Mouncy)
  Loyd 66-68
  see also MARCEANS
MONCELLIS see MONCEAUX
MONCELS see MONCEAUX
MONCEUS see MONCEAUX
MONCHENESY
  1 (Monchenesy)
  2 (Mountchensy)
  5 (Monthensy)
  8 (Hubert de Mont Canisi)
  Hubertus de Montecanisio
    1086 TC
  Hubertus de Monte Canesitu
    /Canisi 1086 ST
  Cleveland II 279-280

MONET see MOUET
MONFICHET
  1 (Monfichet)
  2 (Mounfychet)
  4 (Sire de Monfichet)
  5 (Mounfichet)
  6 (Le sire Mont Fiquet)
  8 (De Montfiquet)
  Cleveland II 266-268
  Loyd 68 (Montfichet)
MONHAUT see MOHANT
MONHERMON
  1 (Monhermon)
  Cleveland II 297-298
    (=Monthermer)
MONNEVILE
  1 (Manuile)
  Nigellus de Monneuile 1086 TC
  Cleveland II 321-322
  see also MANDEVILLE
MONSTIER
  6 (Parnel du Monstier)
MONT CANISI see MONCHENESY
MONT FIQUET see MONFICHET
MONTAGU
  1 (Mountagu)
  2 & 3 & 5 (Montagu)
  7 & 8 (Ansger de Montaigu;
    Dreu de Montaigu)
  Ansgerus de Montagud 1086 TC
  Drogo de Montagud 1086 TC
  Cleveland II 284-293
MONTAGUD see MONTAGU
MONTAIGU see MONTAGU
MONTALENT
  3 (Montalent)
  5 (Mautalent)
  Cleveland III 333-335
    (=Maitland)
MONTALT see MOHANT
MONTBRAI see MOWBRAY
MONTBRAY see MOWBRAY
MONTCHEVREL see MAUNCHENELL
MONTECANISO see MONCHENESY
MONTFICHET see MONFICHET
MONTFOR see MONTFORT
MONTFORD see MONTFORT
MONTFORT
  1 (Mountford)
  2 (Mounford)
  4 (Hue sire de Montfort)
  5 (Mountfort)
  6 (Hue sire de Montfor;
    Le sire de Montfort
    sus Rille)
  7 (Hugue de Montfort

64

le Connestable)
8 (Hugue de Montfort;
  Robert de Montfort)
Hugo de Montefort
  seu Monteforti 1086 TC
Hugo de Montford/Montfort
  1086 ST
Cleveland II 293-295   Loyd 68
Hugh de Montfort, Lord of Montfortsur-Risle, mentioned by William of Poitiers and Orderic, was undoubtedly at the Battle. He was son of Hugh de Montfort I and grandson of Thurstan de Bastenbourg. Orderic styles him Hugh the Constable, and he and his successors undoubtedly held that office [Cf. G.H. White's paper on "Constables under the Norman Kings" in "The Genealogist", N.S. xxxviii, 113-127]. The male line became extinct under Henry I, the later Montforts of this line descending from Hugh II's daughter Alice.
MONTGOMERY
  1 (Mountgomerie)
  4 (Rogier de Montgomeri)
  6 (Roger du Mont Gomery
    Comes)
  7 (Roger de Montgomeri)
  8 (Hugue de Montgomeri;
    Roger de Montgomeri)
  Roger de Montgomery 1086 TC
  Hugo de Montgumeri 1086 TC
  Cleveland II 326-330
  Loyd 68-69
Roger de Montgomery, cousin to Duke William, was left in Normandy and was not present at the Battle, first coming to England with the Conqueror at the end of 1067.
MONTHENSY see MONCHENESY
MONTHERMER see MONHERMON
MONTPINCON see MENPINCOY
MONTRAVERS
  1 & 5 (Montravers)
  3 (Mautrauers)
  Cleveland II 275-277
MONTVILLA see MONVILLE
MONVILLE
  Loyd 69
MOOUN see MOHUN
MORELL
  1 & 3 (Morell)
  Morel 1086 ST
  Cleveland II 304-305
MOREN
  1 (Moren)
  Moran 1086 ST
  Morinus 1086 TC & ST
  Cleveland II 335

MORERS
  Loyd 69
MORES see MURRES
MORETOING see MORTAIN
MORETON see MORTAIN
MOREVILLE see MOREVYLE
MOREVYLE
  2 (Morevyle)
  Loyd 70 (Moreville)
MORIBRAY see MOWBRAY
MORLEIAN see MORLEY
MORLEY
  1 (Morleian)
  3 (Morley)
  5 (Morley; twice)
  Cleveland II 310-312
MORMONT
  6 (Raoult de Mormont)
MORREIS
  1 (Morreis)
  5 (Mourreis)
  Cleveland II 310
MORTAGNE
  7 (Geoffroi, Seigneur
    de Mortagne)
  8 (Mathieu de Mortagne)
Geoffrey of Mortagne, afterwards 1st Count of Perche, mentioned by William of Poitiers and Orderic, was undoubtedly at the Battle. He was son of Rotrou, Count of Mortagne, and fifth in descent from Geoffrey, 1st Vicomte of Chateaudun. His direct descendant, Philip, Count of Perche, was slain at the Battle of Lincoln in 1217, being succeeded by his uncle William, Bishop of Chalons-sur-Marne, the last of the line.
MORTAIN
  1 & 3 (Morton)
  2 (Morten)
  4 (Quens Robert de Moretoing)
  5 (Morteine)
  6 (Robert Earle of Mortaigne)
  7 (Robert Moreton;
    Roger Moreton;
    Robert Comte de Mortain)
  8 (Robert, comte de Mortaine)
  Moritoniensis Comes 1086 TC
  Cleveland II 339-341
Robert, Count of Mortain, afterwards Earl of Cornwall, and younger halfbrother of the Conqueror, is named on the Bayeux Tapestry in the scenes between the landing and the Battle of Hastings and was therefore almost certainly at the Battle.
MORTEINE see MORTAIN
MORTEMER see MORTIMER

MORTEN see MORTAIN
MORTEYNE see MORTAIN
MORTIMAINE
  1 (Mortimaine)
  3 (Mortmaine)
  Cleveland II 255
MORTIMER
  1 (Mortimere)
  2 & 5 (Mortimer)
  4 (Hue de Mortemer)
  6 (Hue de Mortemer)
  7 (Raoul de Mortemer;
    Hugue de Mortemer)
  8 (Raoul de Mortemer)
  Radulfus de Mortemer
    1086 TC & ST
  Cleveland II 248-255
  Loyd 70-71
MORTIUALE
  1 (Mortiuale)
  Cleveland II 278-279
MORTIVAUX
  5 (Mortivaux)
MORTMAINE see MORTIMAINE
MORTON see MORTAIN
MORUILE
  1 & 3 (Moruile)
  5 (Morvile)
  Cleveland II 243-244
  (=Morville)
MORVILLE see MORUILE
MOUBRAY see MOWBRAY
MOUET
  1 (Mouet)
  Cleveland II 320
  (=Monet or Monay)
MOULINOUS see MOLINS
MOULINS see MOLINS
MOUNCELS see MONCEAUX
MOUNCEUS see MONCEAUX
MOUNCY see MONCEAUX
MOUNDEVILE see MANDEVILLE
MOUNFEY
  5 (Mounfey)
  Cleveland III 383 (=Maufe)
  see also MAUFE
MOUNFICHET see MONFICHET
MOUNFORD see MONTFORT
MOUNFYCHET see MONFICHET
MOUNPINSON see MENPINCOY
MOUNS
  2 (Mouns)
MOUNSOREL see MOUNTSOREL
MOUNTABOURS
  2 (Mountabours)
MOUNTAGU see MONTAGU

MOUNTAYN
  2 (Mountayn)
MOUNTBOCHER see MOUNTBOTHER
MOUNTBOTHER
  1 (Mountbother)
  3 (Mountbocher)
  Cleveland II 257-258
MOUNTBURGH
  5 (Mountburgh)
  Cleveland III 383
MOUNTCHAMPE
  2 (Mountchampe)
MOUNTCHENSY see MONCHENESY
MOUNTENEY
  1 (Mounteney)
  3 (Mountney)
  Cleveland II 264-266
MOUNTFORD see MONTFORT
MOUNTFORT see MONTFORT
MOUNTGOMERIE see MONTGOMERY
MOUNTLOUEL
  1 (Mountlouel)
  Cleveland II 323
MOUNTMARTEN
  1 (Mountmarten)
  3 (Mountmartin)
  Cleveland II 315
MOUNTMARTIN see MOUNTMARTEN
MOUNTNEY see MOUNTENEY
MOUNTRIVEL
  5 (Mountrivel)
  Cleveland III 382-383
MOUNTSOLER see MOUNTSOREL
MOUNTSOREL
  1 (Mountsoler)
  2 (Mountsorrell)
  5 (Mounsorel)
  Cleveland II 258-259
MOUNTSORRELL see MOUNTSOREL
MOURREIS see MORREIS
MOUTIERS
  7 (Paisnel des
    Moutiers-Hubert)
  8 (Robert des Moutiers)
MOVET
  5 (Movet)
MOWBRAY
  1 & 3 (Moribray)
  2 (Moubray)
  4 (Cil de Monbrai)
  4 (Giffrei, Eveske
    de Constances)
  5 (Moubray)
  6 (Le sire de Moubray)
  7 (Geoffroi, Eveque de
    Coutances;

Roger de Montbray)
8 (Geoffroi de Montbrai;
Robert de Montbrai)
Cleveland II 235-243
Loyd 71
Geoffrey de Mowbray, Bishop of Coutances, is mentioned by William of Poitiers as being in the expeditionary force to pray and was almost certainly present at the Battle.
MOWNE see MOHUN
MOYAUX
8 (Roger de Moyaux)
MOYON see MOHUN
MUCEDENT
8 (Gautier de Mucedent)
Walterus de Mucedent
1086 ST
MUCELGROS see MUCHEGROS
MUCHEGROS
1 (Musegros)
3 (Musgros)
5 (Mussegros)
7 & 8 (Roger de Mussegros)
Rogerius de Mucelgros
1086 TC
Rogerus de Mucelgros
1086 ST
Cleveland II 269-272
(=Musgrave)
Loyd 71
MUFFET
3 (Muffet)
la MUILE see LAUMALE
De MULLOX
6 (De Mullox)
MUNCELLIS see MONCEAUX
MUNNEVILLE
8 (Neel de Munneville)
MUNPINCUN see MONTPINCON
MURDAC
7 & 8 (Robert Murdac)
MURRES
1 & 3 (Murres)
Cleveland II 278 (=Mores)
MUSARD
1 & 2 & 3 & 5 (Musard)
7 & 8 (Hascouf Musard;
Hugue Musard)
Ascuit/Hascoit/Hasculfus
Musard 1086 TC
Hascoius Musart 1086 TC
Hugo Musardus 1086 TC
Cleveland II 272-273
MUSCAMP see MUSCHAMPE
MUSCHAMPE
3 (Muschampe)

7 (De Muscamp)
Cleveland III 325-326
MUSCHET
5 (Muschet)MUSE
1 & 3 & 5 (Muse)
Cleveland II 255-256
MUSEGRAVE see MUSGRAVE
MUSEGROS see MUCHEGROS
MUSETT
1 (Musett)
Cleveland II 298
MUSGRAUE see MUSGRAVE
MUSGRAVE
2 (Musegrave)
3 (Musgraue)
see also MUCHEGROS
MUSGROS see MUCHEGROS
MUSSEGROS see MUCHEGROS
MUSTEYS
5 (Musteys)
Cleveland III 388-389
MYNERS see MINERS
MYRIET
5 (Myriet)
NAIRMERE see NEIREMET
NARBET
2 (Narbet)
NAZANDA
Loyd 71
NEAUHOU
4 (Sire de Neauhou)
NEBORS
2 (Nebors)
NEELE see NEILE
NEHABON
6 (Le sire de Nehabon)
NEIL see NEILE
NEILE
1 (Neile)
3 (Neele)
4 (Neel de Saint Salveor)
6 (Neel de Saint-Saueur
le vicont)
7 (Neel Vicomte
de St-Sauveur)
8 (Le Vicomte)
Nigel/Nigellus 1086 ST
Cleveland II 360-362
NEIREMET
1 (Neiremet)
5 (Nairmere)
Cleveland II 359-360
NEMBRUTZ
1 (Nembrutz)
Cleveland II 364
NEMUS-ROHARDI see BOSCROARD

67

NENERS
  5 (Neners)
  Cleveland III 395-396
NEOFMARCH
  1 (Neofmarch)
NERBERT see NORBET
NEREVILLE
  2 (Nervyle),
  5 (Nereville)
  Cleveland II 396
NERMITZ
  1 (Nermitz)
  Cleveland II 364
NERVYLE see NEREVILLE
NEUBOURG see NEWBOROUGH
NEUFMARCHE see NEWMARCH
NEUILE see NEVILLE
NEUMARCHE see NEWMARCH
NEUVILLE see NEVILLE
NEVILLE
  1 & 3 (Neuile)
  2 (Nevyle & Knevyle)
  5 (Neville)
  7 (Gilbert de Neuville;
    Richard de Neuville)
  8 (Richard de Neuville)
  Cleveland II 342-351
  Loyd 72-73
NEWBET
  5 (Newbet)
NEWBOROUGH
  1 & 3 (Newborough)
  5 (Newburgh)
  Cleveland II 355-359
  Loyd 72 (Neubourg)
NEWBURGH see NEWBOROUGH
NEWMARCH
  1 & 5 (Newmarch)
  3 (Neumarche)
  7 (Bernard de Neufmarche)
  8 (Bernard du Neufmarche)
  Cleveland II 351-354
  Loyd 72 (Neufmarche)
NIME
  6 (Le sire de Nime)
NOERS
  1 (Noers)
  Willielmus de Noers/Noiers
    1086 ST
  Cleveland II 341-342
  Loyd 74
NOIERS see NOERS
NORBET
  1 & 3 (Norbet)
  Cleveland II 354
    (=Nerbert)

NORECE see NORICE
NORICE
  1 (Norice)
  3 (Norece)
  Cleveland II 354-355
MORMANUILE see MORMANVILLE
NORMANVILLE   1 (Normauile)
  3 (Normanuile)
  Cleveland II 362-364
  Loyd 73-74
NORMAUILE see NORMANVILLE
NORON
  8 (Raoul de Noron)
NORTON
  3 (Norton)
  Cleveland III 336
NOUUERS see NOYERS
NOVO BURGO see NEUBOURG
NOVO MERCATO see NEWMARCH
NOWCHAUMPE
  2 (Nowchaumpe)
NOWERS
  2 (Nowers)
  Loyd 74
  see also NOYERS
NOYERS
  8 (Guillaume de Noyers)
  Willielmus de Nouueres 1086 ST
  Robertus de Nouuers 1086 ST
  Loyd 74
  see also NOWERS
NUERIIS see NOYERS
OBURVILLA see AUBERVILLE
ODBURCUILLA see AUBERVILLE
ODBURGUILLE see AUBERVILLE
ODBURVILE see AUBERVILLE
ODO, Bishop of Bayeux, see BAYEUX
OGLANDER
  7 (Le Sire d'Orglande)
  8 (D'Orglande)
  Loyd 74-75
OILGI see DOYLY
OILLIE see DOYLY
OISELL
  1 (Oisell)
  3 (Oysell)
  5 (Oysel)
  Cleveland II 366
OISTERHAM
  7 (Roger d'Oisterham)
  8 (Roger d'Oistreham)
OLGI see DOYLY
OLIBEF
  1 & 3 (Olibef)
  Cleveland II 364-365
OLIFANT

68

1 (Olifant; Olifard)
3 (Olifaunt; Oliford)
5 (Olifard; Lifford)
Cleveland II 365 & 367-370
& III 382
OLIFARD see OLIFANT
OLIFAUNT see OLIFANT
OLIFORD see OLIFANT
OLYOT
2 (Olyot)
OMFRAVILE see UMFRANVILLE
OMONTVILLE
8 (Gautier d'Omontville)
ONATULE
5 (Onatule)
Cleveland III 396
ONEBAC
4 (Cil d'Onebac)
ORBEC
4 (Dam Richart Orbec)
6 (Richart sire Dorbec)
7 (Richard de Bienfaite
et d'Orbec)
8 (Richard de Bienfaite)
8 (Roger d'Orbec)
Rogerus de Orbec 1086 ST
Loyd 75
ORGLANDE see OGLANDER
ORGLANDRES see OGLANDER
ORIGNY see URINIE
ORINALL
1 (Orinall)
Cleveland II 370 (=Orval)
ORIOLL
1 (Orioll)
3 (Oryoll)
Cleveland II 371 (=Orrell)
ORRELL see ORIOLL
ORVAL see ORINALL
ORYOLL see ORIOLL
OSENEL see OSEVILLE
OSEVILE see OSEVILLE
OSEVILLE
1 (Osenel)
5 (Osevile)
Cleveland II 365-366
Loyd 75
OSMOND
8 (Osmond)
OTBURGUILE see AUBERVILLE
OTBURVILLA see AUBERVILLE
OTENEL
1 (Oteuell)
3 (Otenel)
5 (Otinel)
Cleveland II 364

OTEUELL see OTENEL
OTINEL see OTENEL
OUILLI see DOYLY
OUNFRAVYLE see UMFRANVILLE
OW see EU
OYSEL see OISELL
OYSELL see OISELL
PACEIO see PACY
PACIE see PACY
PACY   4 (Sire de Pacy)
6 (Le sire de Pacy)
7 (Le Sire de Pacy)
Loyd 75-76
PAGANEL see PAYNEL
PAGANEL see PAYNEL
PAIENALS see PAYNEL
PAIFRER see PAIFRERE
PAIFRERE
1 (Paifrere)
5 (Paifrer)
Cleveland III 20-21
(=Peyforer)
PAIGNEL see PAYNEL
PAIGNELL see PAYNEL
PAINELL see PAYNEL
PAISFOR(ERE)
8 (Osberne Pastforeire)
Osbernus Paisfor/Paisforere
/Pastforeire 1086 ST
PAITENY
5 (Paiteny)
Cleveland III 396
PAMPILION see PAMPILIOUN
PAMPILIOUN
1 (Pampilioun)
3 (Pampilion)
5 (Pavillioun)
8 (Turould de Papelion)
Cleveland III 30-31
PANCEVOLT
8 (Bernard Pancevolt)
Bernardus Pancevolt 1086 TC
PANEL see PAYNEL
PANELY see PANILLY
PANILLEUSE, Gerelm de; in a charter of the
Abbey of the Holy Trinity of Rouen a certain
Oger de Panilleuse gave a vineyard to the Abbey,
partly for the salvation of the soul of his brother
Gerelm, lately deceased in England. It is very
likely that Gerelm fought and died in the
Hastings campaign, but as the charter cannot be
dated exactly, it is possible that he was killed in
one of the later campaigns, or died during a
peaceful interval.
PANILLY
2 (Panely)

6 (Le sire de Panilly)
PANTOLF see PANTULF
PANTOUL see PANTULF
PANTULF
1 (Pantolf)
7 (Guillaume de Pantoul)
8 (Guillaume Pantoul)
Cleveland III 38-40
Loyd 76
PAPELION see PAMPILIOUN
PARCHER
Anschitil Parcher 1086 TC
PARIS
8 (Foucher de Paris)
Fulcherus Parisiacensis
1086 ST
PARISIACENSIS see PARIS
PARTENAY
8 (Guillaume de Parthenay)
6 (Le vidam de Partenay)
PARTHENAY see PARTENAY
PASCY see PACY
PASSY
Radulfus Passaq' 1086 ST
PASTFOREIRE see PAISFOR
PATAIS see de la LANDE
PATEFINE
1 (Patefine)
Cleveland III 28-30
PATINE
3 (Patine)
PATRIC see LANDE
PATRY see LANDE
PAUELY see PAVELY
PAUEY
1 (Pauey)
Cleveland II 397-398
PAVELY
1 (Pauely)
5 (Pavely)
Cleveland III 19-20
Loyd 77 (Pavilly)
PAVILLIOUN see PAMPILIOUN
PAVILLY see PAVELY
PAYNEL
1 (Painell)
2 (Paynell)
3 (Paynel)
4 (Paienals des
Monstiers-Hubert),
5 (Panel alias Paignel)
8 (Raoul Painel)
Radulfus Pagenel 1086 TC
Cleveland II 390-395
Loyd 77
PECCELL

1 (Peccell)
PECHE see PERCHE
PECY
3 (Pecy)
PEITO
1 (Peito)
7 (Gautier Le Poitevin;
Guillaume Le Poitevin;
Roger Le Poitevin)
8 (Guillaume Le Poitevin;
Roger Le Poitevin)
Cleveland III 40-42
(=Poitou)
PEIZ see DEPEIZ
PEKENEY see PINKENEY
PEKENY see PINKENEY
PENBRI
2 (Penbri)
PENECORD
1 (Penecord)
3 (Penicord)
see also VENICORDE
& FAUECOURT
PENICORD see PENECORD
PERAPUND see PEREPOUNT
PERCEHAY see PERCY
PERCELAY see PERCY
PERCEVAL see PERCIUALE
PERCHE
1 (Perche)
3 (Peche)
5 (Peche)
7 (Guillaume Peche)
8 (Guillaume Peche; Geoffroi,
comte de la Perche)
Cleveland II 395-397
(=Peche)
PERCI see PERCY
PERCIUALE
1 (Perciuale)
Cleveland III 45-47
(=Perceval)
PERCY
1 (Percelay)
2 (Percy)
5 (Percy; Percehay)
7 (Guillaume de Percy)
8 (Arnoul de Perci;
Guillaume de Perci)
Radulfus Percehaie 1086 TC
Willielmus de Perci
1086 TC & ST
Cleveland III 31-32
Loyd 77
see also PERY
PERECOUNT

3 (Perecount)
PEREPOUNT
  1 (Perepount)
  5 (Perpounte)
  7 (Geoffroi de Pierrepont;
    Robert de Pierrepont)
  8 (Geoffroi de Pierrepont;
    Renaud de Pierrepont;
    Robert de Pierrepont)
  Reinaldus de Perapund
    1086 ST
  Cleveland II 381-386
    (=Pierrepont)
  Loyd 78 (Pierrepont)
PERERE
  1 (Perere)
  5 (Pereris; Perrers)
  Cleveland III 32-34
PERERIS see PERERE
PEROT
  1 & 3 & 5 (Perot)
  Cleveland III 5-7
PERPOUNTE see PEREPOUNT
PERRERS see PERERE
PERSHALE
  1 & 3 (Pershale)
  Cleveland II 386-387
PERTENAI
  W. de Pertenai 1086 ST
PERWINKE
  3 (Perwinke)
  Cleveland III 340-341
PERY
  1 (Pery)
  Cleveland II 374-381
    (=Percy)
  see also PERCY
PETIUOLL
  1 (Petiuoll)
  Cleveland III 36
PETROPONTE see PIERREPONT
PEUERELL see PEVEREL
PEUKENEY see PINKENY
PEURELL see PEVEREL
PEVEREL
  1 (Peurell)
  2 (Peverell)
  3 (Peuerell)
  5 (Peverel; Peverelle)
  7 (Guillaume Pevrel)
  8 (Guillaume Pevrel;
    Renouf Pevrel)
  Will(i)elmus Peverel/
    Piperellus 1086 TC & ST
  Ran(n)ulfus Peverell/
    Piperellus 1086 TC & ST

  Cleveland III 1-5
PEVERELLE see PEVEREL
PEVREL see PEVEREL
PEYFORER see PAIFRERE
PEYNS
  2 (Peyns)
PEYVERE
  2 (Peyvere)
PHAIRE see PHUARS
PHUARS
  1 (Phuars)
  Cleveland III 23-24 (=Phaire)
PICARD 1 & 3 (Picard)
  5 (Pikard; Pykarde)
  Rogerus Pictaviensis 1086 TC
  Cleveland III 7-8
PICOT see PIGOT
PICQUIGNI see PINKENY
PIERREPONT see PEREPOUNT
PIGOT
  1 & 3 (Pigot)
  5 (Pygot)
  7 & 8 (Roger Picot)
  Rogerus Picot 1086 ST
  Cleveland II 371-374
PIKARD see PICARD
PIMERAY see POMERAY
PINCERNA
  Hugo Pincerna 1086 TC
  Ricardus Pincerna 1086 ST
PINCHARD
  1 (Pinchard)
  3 (Pynchard)
  Cleveland III 25-26
PINCHENGI see PINKENY
PINEL see PINELL
PINELL
  1 (Pinell)
  8 (Raoul Pinel)
  Radulfus Pinel/Pinellus
    1086 TC & ST
  Cleveland III 35
PINKADOUN
  5 (Pinkadoun)
PINKENIE see PINKENY
PINKENY
  1 (Peukeney; Pinkenie;
    Pekeny)
  2 (Pynkeney)
  3 (Pekeney)
  5 (Pinkeney)
  6 (Le sire de Piqgny)
  7 (Anscoul de Picquigni;
    Giles de Picquigni;
    Guillaume de Picquigni)
  8 (Anscoul de Picquigni;

Guillaume de Picquigni)
Ansculfus de & Willielmus
  Pinchengi 1086 ST
  Cleveland III 8-9
  Loyd 78
PINS
  4 (Sire des Pins)
  6 (Le sire de Pins)
  7 (Le Sire de Pins)
PIPEREL see PEVEREL
PIPIN
  8 (Raoul Pipin)
  Radulfus Pipin 1086 ST
PIQGNY see PINKENYPIRON
  6 (Le sire de Piron)
PIROU
  4 (Chevalier de Pirou)
  7 (Le Chevalier de Pirou)
PISTRES
  8 (Roger de Pistres)
PLACE
  1 (Place)
  Cleveland III 29-30 (=Playz)
PLACY
  1 & 3 (Placy)
  Cleveland III 26
de la PLANCH see DELAPLANCH
PLAYZ see PLACE
PLUKENET
  1 & 5 (Plukenet)
  Cleveland III 21-23 (=Plunket)
PLUNKET see PLUKENET
POER see POWER
POIGNANT see POINGIANT
POILLEI see POILLGI
POILLGI
  8 (Guillaume de Poillei)
  Willelmus de Poillgi 1086 TC
POINGIANT
  8 (Guillaume Poignant;
    Richard Poignant)
  Ricardus Poingiant/Puingiant
    /Pugnant/Pungiant
    1086 ST & TC
POINTEL
  7 & 8 (Thierri Pointel)
  Tedricus Pointel/Puintel
    1086 TC & ST
Le POITEVIN see PEITO
POIS
  8 (Guernon de Pois)
POITOU see PEITO
de la POLE see DELAPOLE
POMERAI see POMERAY
POMERAY
  1 & 2 (Pomeray)

3 (Pimeray)
7 (Raoul de la Pommeraie)
8 (Raoul de La Pommeraie)
Radulfus de Pomerei
  1086 TC & ST
  Cleveland III 9-12
  Loyd 78-79 (Pomerai)
POMERIA see POMERAY
la POMMERAYE see POMERAY
PONTCARDS see PUNCHARDIN
PONCHARDIN see PUNCHARDIN
PONS see POUNCE
PONT-DE-L'ARCHE
  8 (Guillaume de Pont-de-l'Arche)
PONTCHARDON see PUNCHARDIN
PONTE CARDONIS see PUNCHARDIN
PONTHER
  Walterus Ponther 1086 ST
PONTHIEU; a Latin poem on the Battle of
Hastings, attributed to Guy, Bishop of Amiens from
1058 to 1076, relates how near the end of the battle
the body of the dying Harold was mutilated by four
men, three of whom were undoubtedly at the battle.
The fourth is not named, being mentioned vaguely
as the noble heir of Ponthieu. There are
considerable problems in the identification of this
man and the whole incident, which is ignored by the
best authorities, is dismissed as fiction by G.H.
White.
PORT
  4 (Cil de Port)
  6 (Le sire de Port)
  7 (Hubert de Port;
    Hugues de Port)
  8 (Hubert de Port; Hugue de Port)
  Hugo de Porth/Port
    1086 TC & ST
  Hubertus de Porth 1086 TC
  Loyd 79-80
PORTES
  Loyd 80-81
PORTH see PORT
PORTMORT
  Loyd 81
POTERELL
  1 & 3 (Poterell)
POTERIA
  Loyd 81-82
POUNCE
  1 (Pounce)
  2 (Pounsey)
  5 (Poynce)
  Drogo filius Ponz 1086 TC
  Drogo f. Ponzii 1086 ST
  Cleveland III 12-19
    (=Pons=Clifford=Poyntz)

72

POUNCHARDON see PUNCHARDIN
POUNSEY see POUNCE
POUNTLARGE
  2 (Pountlarge)
POUTREL see PUTRILL
POWER
  1 & 3 & 5 (Power)
  7 (Le Sire de Poer)
  Cleveland II 387-390
  (=Power & Poer)
POYNCE see POUNCE
POYNINGS
  Loyd 82-83
POYNTZ see POUNCE
PRAELS see PREAUX
PRAERES see PRAERS
PRAERS
  4 (Sire de Praeres)
  6 (Le sire de Praores)
  7 (Le Sire de Praeres)
  Cleveland III 36-38
  (=Praers)
  Loyd 83 (Praeres)
PRAORES see PRAERS
PRAUX see PREAUX
PREAUS see PREAUX
PREAUX
  1 (Preaus)
  4 (Cil de Praels)
  6 (Le sire de Praux)
  7 (Eudes Dapifer,
    Sire de Preaux)
  Cleveland III 36-38
PRENDERGAST see PREUDIRLEGAST
PREUDIRLEGAST
  1 (Preudirlegast)
  Cleveland III 42-45
  (=Prendergast)
PUDSEY
  3 (Pudsey)
  Cleveland III 336-340
PUGOY
  1 (Pugoy)
  5 (Pugoys)
  Cleveland III 26-28
PUGOYS see PUGOY
PUNCHARDIN
  1 (Punchardoun)
  2 (Pounchardon)
  3 (Punchardon)
  8 (Robert de Pontchardon)
  Robertus de Pont cardon 1086 ST
  Loyd 83 (Punchardon)
PUNCHARDON see PUNCHARDIN
PUNCHARDOUN see PUNCHARDIN
PUTRILL

  1 (Putrill)
  Cleveland III 35-36
  (=Poutrell)
PYGOT see PIGOT
PYKARDE see PICARD
PYNCHARD see PINCHARD
PYNKENEY see PINKENY
PYPARD
  2 (Pypard)
PYPOTTE
  2 (Pypotte)
PYRYTON
  2 (Pyryton)
QUERCU see QUERRU
QUERRU 5 (Querru)
  Cleveland III 396 (=Quercu)
QUILLI
  Loyd 84
QUINCI see QUINCY
QUINCY
  1 (Quinci)
  2 (Quiney)
  3 & 5 (Quincy)
  Cleveland III 47-49
  Loyd 84
QUINEY see QUINCY
QUINTIN see QUINTINE
QUINTINE
  1 (Quintiny)
  3 (Quintine)
  Cleveland III 49-50
  (=Quintin)
  see also ST. QUINTIN
QUINTINY see QUINTINE
RABAND
  1 (Raband)
  Cleveland III 70 (=Rabayne)
RABAYNE see RABAND
RAIMBEAUCOURT see RAINBUEDCURT
RAIMES
  7 & 8 (Roger de Rames)
  Roger(i)us de Rames/Ramis
  1086 TC & ST
  Loyd 84
RAIMOND
  1 (Raimond)
  3 (Reymond)
  Cleveland III 85-86
RAINBUEDCURT
  8 (Enguerrand de Raimbeaucourt;
    Gui de Raimbeaucourt)
  Wido de Rainbuedcourt/
    Rembudcurt/
    Reinbuedcurt 1086 TC
  Ingelrannus filius Widonis
    de Reinbuedcurt 1086 ST

73

RAINECOURT
8 (Gui de Rainecourt)
RAINES see REINES
RAINEVILLE
Loyd 84
see also RINUILL
RAIT
1 (Rait)
Cleveland III 79
RAMES see RAIMES
RANDUILE
1 (Randuile)
Cleveland III 76
(=Rodeville)
RASTOKE
1 (Rastoke)
Cleveland III 77
RAVENOT
8 (Ravenot)
REBERCIL
4 (Sire de Rebercil)
6 (Le sire de Roberchil)
7 (Le Sire de Rebercil)
REDNES see REINES
REDVERS
4 (Sire de Reviers)
7 & 8 (Guillaume de Reviers;
Richard de Reviers)
Ricardus de Redvers 1086 TC
Loyd 85 (Reviers)
see also RIVERS
REINBUEDCURT see RAINBUEDCURT
REINES
Loyd 84
REINERVILLE see RAINEVILLE
REINEVILLE see RAINEVILLE
REMBUDCURT see RAINBUEDCURT
RENNES
8 (Hugue de Rennes)
RETNES see REINES
REVEL see RIUELL
REVIERS see REDVERS
REYMOND see RAIMOND
REYNEVIL
5 (Reynevil)
RHUDDLAN
8 (Robert de Rhuddlan)
Robertus de Roelent 1086 TC
Robertus de Roelent/
Rodelend/
Rodelent 1086 ST
Loyd 85
RICARDVILE see RICARVILLE
RICARVILLE
Loyd 86
RICHARDIVILLA see RICARDVILLE

RICHEMOUND see RICHMOND
RICHER see RISERS
RICHFORD
2 (Richford)
RICHMOND
1 (Richemound)
3 (Richmond)
7 (Le Comte Alain Le Noir;
Le Comte Alain Le Roux)
Cleveland III 81-84
RIDEL
1 (Ridell)
3 (Ridle)
5 (Ridel)
7 (Geoffroi Ridel)
Cleveland III 57-59
RIDELL see RIDEL
RIDLE see RIDELRIE
1 (Rie)
7 (Adam de Rie; Hubert de
Rie; Raoul de Rie)
Cleveland III 71-75
RIGNY
1 (Rigny)
Cleveland III 80
RIMER
6 (Le sire de la Rimer)
RINUILL
1 (Rinuill)
Cleveland III 77-78
(=Reinevile)
see also RAINEVILLE
RIPERE
1 & 5 (Ripere)
7 (Le Sire de Rupierre)
Cleveland III 79
(=Rupierre=Roper)
RISBOIL
8 (Gautier de Risbou)
Galt. de Risboil 1086 ST
RISBOU see RISBOIL
RISERS
1 (Risers)
5 (Rysers)
Cleveland III 76 (=Richer)
RIUEIRE see RIVERS
RIUELL
1 (Riuell)
2 (Rivel)
3 (Rynel)
5 (Ryvel & Revel)
Cleveland III 62-63
(=Revell)
RIUERS see RIVERS
RIVERS
1 (Riuers)

74

2 (Rivers)
5 (Rivers & De la Rivers;
  Ryvers)
6 (Le sire de Riuers)
8 (Goscelin de La Riviere)
Gozelinus Riueire 1086 TC
Cleveland III 59-62
see also REDVERS
RIVIERE see RIVERS
ROBERCHIL see REBERCIL
ROBERT
  6 (Hubert Robert)
ROCHEFORD see ROCHFORD
ROCHFORD
  1 (Rochford)
  [2 (Richford)]
  3 (Rocheford)
  Cleveland III 85
RODES   2 (Rodes)
RODEVILLE see RANDUILE
ROELENT see RHUDDLAN
ROGER son of TUROLD; Roger, son of Turold,
when about to voyage overseas with Count
William, made a gift to the Abbey of the Holy
Trinity at Rouen; but because he could not
confirm it, being prevented by death in the same
voyage (navigatione), a certain knight of his did
so. This is clear proof that Roger started on the
Expedition of 1066; but we are left in doubt as to
whether he died before or after the Battle of
Hastings or was killed in the Battle. Strictly
navigatione would imply that he died at sea, but
it would be rash to insist on this literal
translation.
ROGERS see ROUGERE
ROKELL
  1 & 5 (Rokell)
  Cleveland III 75-76
ROLLOS
  Loyd 86
ROMARE
  4 (Dam Willame de Romare)
  6 (Guilliam sire de Romare)
  7 (Guillaume de Roumare)
  Loyd 87 (Roumare)
ROMENEL
  8 (Robert de Romenel)
  Ro(t)bertus de Romenel
    1086 TC & ST
ROMELY
  6 (Le sire de Romely)
  Loyd 87 (Rumilly)
ROND see RONDE
RONDE
  1 (Ronde)
  3 (Rond)

Cleveland III 71
ROPER see RIPERE
ROS
  1 & 5 (Ros)
  2 & 3 (Rose)
  7 (Ansgot de Ros; Anquetil de
    Ros; Guillaume de Ros)
  8 (Anquetil de Ros; Ansgot de
    Ros; Geoffroi de Ros;
    Serlo de Ros)
  Anschitillus/Ansgotus/
    Goisfridus/
  Serlo de Ros 1086 ST
  Cleveland III 50-57
  Loyd 86
ROSAI see ROSEIROSE see Ros
ROSEI
  8 (Vauquelin de Rosai)
  Loyd 86-87
ROSEL see RUSSEL
ROSELIN
  1 (Roselin)
  5 (Roscelin)
  Rozelinus homo Comitis
    Hugonis 1086 ST
  Cleveland III 76
ROSETO see ROSEI
ROUGERE
  1 (Rougere)
  Cleveland III 78-79
  (=Rogers)
ROUMARE see ROMARE
ROUS
  1 & 3 (Rous)
  Hugo Rufus 1086 ST
  Cleveland III 63-65
ROUSSEL see RUSSEL
ROUX
  8 (Alain Le Roux)
ROVILLE
  Loyd 87
ROSCELIN see ROSELIN
RUGETIUS
  5 (Rugetius)
  Cleveland III 397
RUILI
  Loyd 87
RULLOS see ROLLOS
RUMILLY see ROMELY
RUNEVILLE see RUNEUILE
RUNEUILE
  8 (Geoffroi de Runeville)
  Goisfr' Runeuile 1086 ST
RUPIERRE see RIPERE
RUSHELL see RUSSEL
RUSSEL

1 (Rushell)
3 (Russel)
5 (Rosel)
7 (Hugue de Roussel)
Cleveland III 65-70
RY
  5 (Ry)
RYNEL see RIUELL
RYSERS see RISERS
RYVEL see RIUEL
RYVERS see RIVERS
SACHEVEREL see ST. CHEUEROLL
SACHEVILLA see SAGEVILLE
SACIE see SACY
SACKVILLE
  Loyd 88
SACQUENVILLE see SAGEVILLESACY
  4 (Cil de Sacie)
  6 (Le sire de Sacy;
    Le Sire de Saussay)
  7 (Osberne de Sassy;
    Raoul de Sassy)
  8 (Osberne de Saussai;
    Raoul de Saussai)
  Loyd 95 (Saucy)
  see also SALCEIT and SAUNCEY
SAGEVILLE
  5 (Sageville)
  8 (Richard de Sacquenville)
  Ricardus de Sacheuilla
    1086 ST
  Cleveland III 398-399
  Loyd 88 (Sachevilla)
SAI see SAY
SAIE see SAY
ST. ALBIN
  1 (St. Albin)
  2 (St. Aubyn)
  3 (St. Albine)
  Cleveland III 129-131
ST. ALBINE see ST. ALBIN
ST. AMAND
  1 (St. Amond)
  2 (St. Amauns)
  3 (St. Amand)
  5 (twice; Sainct Amande)
  Cleveland III 99-100
ST. AMANDE see ST. AMAND
ST. AMARY
  5 (St. Amary)
ST. AMAUNS see ST. AMAND
ST. AMOND see ST. AMAND
ST. AUBYN see ST. ALBIN
ST. AUDOENO see ST. OUEN
ST. BARBE
  1 & 3 & 5 (St. Barbe)

Cleveland III 134-136
ST. CHEUEROLL
  1 (St. Cheueroll)
  Cleveland III 139-142
  (=Sacheverel)
ST. CLAIR
  1 (Senclere)
  2 (St. Cler)
  4 (Cil de Saint Cler)
  5 (St. Clere)
  6 (Le sire de Sainct-Cler)
  7 (Richard de St-Clair)
  8 (Richard de Saint Clair)
  Richardus de Sencler/
    Sent Cler 1086 ST
  Loyd 88-89 (Sancto Claro)
  Cleveland III 91-96
ST. CLER(E) see ST. CLAIR
ST. CLO
  2 (St. Lou)
  3 (St. Clo)
  Cleveland III 341-343
  (=St. Lo)
ST. CLOYIS
  5 (St. Cloyis)
  Cleveland III 397
ST. CRISTOFORO
  Loyd 93
St. DENIS
  2 (St. Denis)
SAINTEALS see CINTHEAUX
SAINTEAULX see CINTHEAUX
ST. FOY
  Loyd 93 (Sancta Fide)
ST. FYLBERT
  2 (St. Fylbert)
ST. GALERI see ST. VALERY
ST. GEORGE
  1 & 3 (St. George)
  Cleveland III 121
ST. GERMAIN see ST. GERMANS
ST. GERMANS
  7 (Roger de St-German)
  8 (Roger de Saint Germain)
  Rogerus de Sancto Germano
    1086 ST
  Loyd 94 (Sancto Germano)
ST. HELEN
  8 (Renaud de Sainte Helene;
    Toustain de Sainte Helene)
ST. HILAIRE
  Loyd 89 (Sancto Hilario)
ST. IEHAN see ST. JOHN
ST. IOHN see ST. JOHN
ST. JAY
  2 (St. Jay)

ST. JEAN see ST. JOHN
ST. JOHAN see ST. JOHN
ST. JOHN
  1 (St. John)
  2 (St. Johan)
  4 (Cels de Saint Johan)
  5 (St. John)
  6 (Le sire de Sainct-Iehan)
  7 (Guillaume de St-Jean)
  Cleveland III 116-121
  Loyd 89-90 (Sancto Johanne)
ST. JORY
  5 (St. Jory)
  Cleveland III 397 (=Jory)
ST. LAURENT
  Loyd 90 (Sancto Laurentio)
ST. LEGER
  1 (St. Legere)
  2 & 3 (St. Leger)
  5 (St. Ligiere)
  7 (Robert de St-Leger)
  8 (Robert de Saint Leger)
  Robertus S. Leger 1086 ST
  Cleveland III 100-103
  Loyd 90 (Sancto Leodegario)
ST. LEGERE see ST. LEGER
ST. LEO
  5 (St. Leo)
ST. LES
  1 & 3 (St. Les)
  Cleveland III 121-124
  (=St Liz)
  see also SENLIS
ST. LIGIERE see ST. LEGER
ST. LIZ see ST. LES
ST. LO see ST. CLO
ST. LOU see ST. CLO
ST. MALOU
  2 (St. Malou)
ST. MANEVO
  Loyd 94 (Sancto Manevo)
ST. MARIE D'AGNEAUX
  8 (De Sainte Marie d'Agneaux)
ST. MARTIN
  1 & 2 (St. Martin)
  4 (Sire de Saint-Martin)
  5 (St. Martine)
  6 (Le Sire de Sainct-Martin)
  7 (Le Sire de St-Martin)
  Cleveland III 131-133
  Loyd 90-91 (Sancto Martino)
ST. MERE EGLISE
  Loyd 93 (Sancte
    Marie Ecclesia)
ST. MOR see ST. MORE
ST. MORE

1 (St. More)
2 (St. Mor)
3 & 5 (St. More)
Cleveland III 142-149
  (=Seymour)
ST. OMER
  1 (St. Omere)
  2 & 3 (St. Omer)
  Cleveland III 96-99
ST. OUEN
  7 (Bernard de St-Ouen)
  8 (Bernard de Saint Ouen)
  Bernardus de Sancto Audoeno
    1086 ST
  Loyd 91 (Sancto Audoeno)
ST. PER
  2 (St. Per)
ST. PLANEES
  Loyd 94 (Sancto Planees)
ST. QUINTIN
  1 (St. Quintin)
  2 (St. Quinteyn)
  3 & 5 (St. Quintine)
  7 (Hugue de St-Quentin)
  8 (Hugue de Saint Quentin)
  Hugo S. Quintini 1086 TC
  Cleveland III 96-98
  Loyd 92
ST. QUINTINE see ST. QUINTIN
ST. SAEN
  6 (Le Sire de Sainct-Saen)
ST. SALVEOR see NEILE
ST. SANSON
  8 (Raoul de Saint Sanson)
  Radulfus de S. Sansone
    1086 ST
ST. SAVIOUR see NEILE
ST. SCUDEMOR see ST. SCUDEMORE
ST. SCUDEMORE
  1 (St. Scudemore)
  3 (St. Scudemor)
  Cleveland III 149-152
ST. SEVER
  4 (Seignor de Saint-Sever)
  7 (Le Sire de St-Sever)
ST. TESE
  5 (St. Tese)
ST. THOMER
  5 (St. Thomer)
ST. VALERY
  2 (St. Walry)
  4 (Sire de Saint Galeri)
  6 (Le Sire de Sainct-Wallery)
  7 (Bernard de St-Valery)
  8 (Gautier de Saint Valeri;
    Renouf de Saint Valeri)

Walterius de Sancto
  Waleri/Walerico 1086 TC
  Loyd 92 (Sancto Walarico)
ST. VELERY see ST. VALERY
ST. VIGOR
  2 (St. Vigor)
ST. VILE
  1 (St. Vile)
  Cleveland III 136
  (=Sandvile)
  see also SANDERVILLE
ST. WALERI(CO) see ST. VALERY
ST. WALLERY see ST. VALERY
ST. WALRY see ST. VALERY
SALCEID see SALCEIT
SALCEIT
  Osbernus de Salceid 1086 TC
  Radulphus de Salceit 1086 TC
  Loyd 93 (Salceit)
  see also SACY
SALLIGNY
  6 (Le sire de Salligny)
SALNARINLLE
  6 (Le sire de Salnarinlle)
SALNERVILLE see SANDERVILLE
SALVAYN see SALVIN
SALVIN
  1 (Saluin)
  5 (Salvayn)
  Cleveland III 124-126
SALUIN see SALVIN
SANCTES
  1 (Sanctes)
  Cleveland III 109
SANCY see SAUNCEY
SANDERVILLE
  1 (Sanduile)
  3 (Sandeuile)
  Cleveland III 137
  Loyd 94-95
  see also ST. VILE
SANDEUILE see SANDERVILLE
SANDUILE see SANDERVILLE
SANFORD
  1 & 3 (Sanford)
  2 (Saunford)
  5 (Saunford)
  Cleveland III 108-109
SANSON
  8 (Sanson)
SANZAYER see SAUNSOUERE
SAP
  4 (Cil de Sap)
  6 (Le Sire de Sap)
  7 (Baudoin de Meules
    et du Sap)

SARTILLY
  Loyd 95
SASSY see SACY
SAUAY
  1 (Sauay)
  Cleveland III 109
SAUCY see SACY
SAUINE see SAVENIE
SAULAY
  1 (twice; Saulay)
  Cleveland III 110-111
  (=Sully)
SAUNCEY
  1 (Sauncey)
  6 (Le sire de Sancy)
  Cleveland III 137-138
  see also SACY
SAUNFORD see SANFORD
SAUNSOUERE
  1 (Sanzayer)
  5 (Saunzaver)
  Cleveland III 107
SAUNZAVER see SAUNSOUERE
SAUNZPOUR
  5 (Saunzpour)
  Cleveland III 398
SAUSSAY see SACY
SAUVAGE
  2 (Sauvage)
SAUVAY
  5 (Sauvay)
SAVENIE
  3 (Sauine)
  8 (Raoul de Savigni)
  Radulfus de Sauigni/Sauenie/
    Sau'gno/Sauigneio/
    Sauigniaco 1086 ST
  Loyd 95
SAVIGNI see SAVENIE
SAVIGNO see SAVENIE
SAY
  1 & 2 & 5 (Say)
  4 (Cil de Saie)
  6 (Le sire de Say)
  7 (Picot de Saye;
    Guillaume Saye)
  Cleveland III 126-128
  Loyd 96
SAYE see SAY
SCALERS or SCALIER see CHALEYS
SCALES see CHALEYS
SCOHIES see ESCOIS
SCORCHEBOFE
  Loyd 96
SCOTEIGNY see SCOTNEY
SCOTENI see SCOTNEY

78

SCOTNEY
 Loyd 96-97
SCOUTEUILLE
 6 (Le sire de Scouteuille)
SCROPE
 3 (Lescrope)
 Osbernus filius Ricardi
  Scrope/Scrupe 1086 TC
 Cleveland III 311-318
SCRUPE see SCROPE
SCUDAMORE see ST. SCUDEMORE
SCUDET or SCUTET
 Will(i)elmus Scudet/Scutet
  1086 TC & ST
SCURES
 Loyd 97
SEGUIN
 1 (Seguin)
 5 (Sengryn)
 Cleveland III 134
SEMILLIE see SEMILLY
SEMILLY
 4 (Sire de Semillie)
 6 (Le sire de Semilly)
 7 (Guillaume de Semilly)
SENARPONT
 8 (Ansger de Senarpont)
SENCLERE see ST. CLAIR
SENESCHAL
 8 (Eude Le Seneschal;
  Hamon Le Seneschal)
SENGRYN see SEGUIN
SENLIS
 7 & 8 (Simon de Senlis)
 see also ST. LES
SEPTEM MOLENDINIS see SEPT MEULES
SEPTEM MOLIS see SEPT MEULES
SEPT MEULES
 8 (Guillaume de Sept Meules)
 Loyd 97-98
SESEE see SESSE
SESSE
 1 (Sesse)
 5 (Sesee)
 Cleveland III 124
SEUCHE see SOUCH
SEUCHEUS
 1 (Seucheus)
 6 (Le sire de Seukee)
 Cleveland III 91
SEUKEE see SEUCHEUS
SEVELE see SHEUILE
SEWARD see SIWARD
SEYMOUR see ST. MORE
SHEUILE
 1 (Sheuile)

Cleveland III 90-91
 (=Sevele)
SILVESTRE
 8 (Hugue Silvestre)
SIFREWAST see SIREWAST
SIREWAST
 1 (Sirewast)
 Cleveland III 138-139
 (=Sifrewast)
 Loyd 98 (Sifrewast)
SIWARD
 1 (Siward)
 2 (Seward)
 Cleveland III 106-107
SMALAVILLA see ESMALEVILLA
SOLENNEI see SOLNEY
SOLERS
 1 & 5 (Solers)
 Cleveland III 128-129
SOLIGNIE see SOLNEY
SOLNEY
 4 (Sire de Solignie)
 7 (Le Sire de Soligny)
 Loyd 98
SOMERAYE see SOMEREY
SOMEREY
 1 (Somerey)
 2 & 3 (Somery)
 5 (Somery; Someraye)
 8 (Roger de Sommeri)
 Rogerus de Sumeri 1086 ST
 Cleveland III 114-116
SOMERUILE
 1 (Someruile)
 3 (Soueruile)
 Cleveland III 103-106
SOMERY see SOMEREY
SOMMERI see SOMEREY
SOREGLISE
 1 (Soreglise)
 Cleveland III 137
SOREL
 1 (Sorell)
 5 (Sorel)
 Cleveland III 113
SORELL see SOREL
SOTEUILE
 6 (Le sire de Soteuile)
SOUCH
 1 (Souch)
 3 (Seuche)
 Cleveland III 86-90
 (=Zouche)
SOUCHEVILLE
 5 (Soucheville)
 Cleveland III 398

79

SOUERUILE see SOMERUILE
SOULES
  5 (Soules)
SOULEY
  5 (Souley)
SOURDEMALE
  1 (Sourdemale)
  Cleveland III 133-134
  see also SURDEVAL
SOUREMOUNT
  1 (Souremount)
  Cleveland III 136
SOVERENG
  5 (Sovereng)
  Cleveland III 397
SPECH
  Willelmus Spech 1086 TC
SPENSER
  2 (Spenser)
SPINAY
  6 (Le sire de Spinay)
SPINEVILLA
  Loyd 98
STAFFORD
  Loyd 99
STOKES
  2 (Stokes)
STOTEVYLE see ESTOUTEVILLE
STRABO
  Loyd 99
STRAUNGE 2 (Straunge)
STUR
  Loyd 99 (William son of)
SULES
  1 (Sules)
  Cleveland III 111-113
SULIGNEI see SOLNEY
SULLY see SAULAY
SURDEVAL
  5 (Surdevale)
  7 & 8 (Richard de Sourdeval)
  Ricardus de Surdeual 1086 TC
  Loyd 99
  see also SOURDEMALE
SURDEVALE see SURDEVAL
SUMERI see SOMEREY
SUYLLY
  5 (Suylly)
TAHUM
  Loyd 100
TAILLEBOIS
  3 (Talybois)
  7 & 8 (Guillaume Taillebois)
    Ive Taillebois;
    Raoul Taillebois)
  Willelmus Tailgebosch 1086 TC

Ivo Taillgebosc/
  Tallebosc 1086 TC
Radulfus Talgebosc/
  Talliebosc 1086 ST
  Cleveland III 344-349
  Loyd 100
TAILLEFER
  4 (Taillefer)
  7 (Taillefer)
From a Latin poem on the Battle of Hastings,
attributed to Guy, Bishop of Amiens from 1058 to
1076, is derived the account of the opening of the
battle by the exploits of a minstrel (histrio)
nicknamed 'Incisor Ferri', who went before the
Norman host and continued singing and juggling
with his sword until he was slain. G.H. White
considered him fictitious.
TAISSEL
  Wimundus de Taissel 1086 ST
  Loyd 100
TAISSON
  Loyd 101
TAKEL
  5 (Takel)
  Cleveland III 408-409
TAKET
  1 & 3 (Taket)
  Cleveland III 159TALBOT
  1 (Talbot)
  2 (Talbote)
  3 & 5 (Talbot)
  7 (Geoffroi Talbot; Guillaume
    Talbot; Richard Talbot)
  8 (Geoffroi Talbot;
    Richard Talbot)
  Goisfridus/Ricardus Talebot
    1086 ST
  Cleveland III 164-171
  Loyd 100
TALLY
  5 (Tally)
  6 (Le sire de Tilly)
  7 (Raoul de Tilly)
  8 (De Tilly)
  Cleveland III 399-400
  (=Tilly)
  Loyd 103-104 (Tilly)
TALYBOIS see TAILLEBOIS
TANCARVILLE
  1 (Tankeruile)
  4 (Chamberlene de
    Tancharvile)
  6 (Le sire de Tankeruille)
  7 (Le Chamberlain de
    Tancarville)
  Cleveland III 194-197

80

Loyd 101
TANCHARVILE see TANCARVILLE
TANI see TANNY
TANIE see TANNY
TANKERUILE see TANCARVILLE
TANKERUILLE see TANCARVILLE
TANNY
  1 & 3 (Tanny)
  5 (Tany)
  8 (Auvrai de Tanie)
  Cleveland III 183
  Loyd 101 (Tani)
TANY see TANNY
TARDEUILE
  1 (Tardeuile)
  Cleveland III 204
TARTERAY see CATERAY
TAUERNER see TAVERNER
TAUERS
  3 (Tauers)
  Cleveland III 349
  see also TRAUERS
TAVERNER
  1 & 3 (Tauerner)
  Cleveland III 192
TAY
  5 (Tay)
TEDBOLDVILLA see TIBOUVILLA
TEISSON see TESSON
TENWIS
  1 (Tenwis)
  Cleveland III 205-206
  (=Tingez)
TERCY
  1 (Tercy)
  Cleveland III 152
TERRY GUASTA see TERRA VASTA
TERRA VASTA
  Loyd 101
TESSEL
  8 (Guimond de Tessel)
TESSON
  1 (Trison)
  4 (Baron Raol Teisson
    de Cingueleiz)
  6 (Raoul Tesson
    de Chignelois)
  7 (Raoul Tesson)
  Cleveland III 162-164
  Loyd 101-102
  see also CONCHES
THAON
  8 (Robert Thaon)
THAYS
  5 (Thays)
  see also TRAIES

THEIL
  8 (Raoul de Theil)
THORNILLE
  5 (Thornille)
THORNY
  2 (Tornay)
  5 (Thorny)
  8 (Geoffroi de Tournai)
  Goisfridus Tornai 1086 ST
  Cleveland III 405
THOUARS
  4 (Visquens de Toarz)
  6 (Almary de Touaers;
    Le vicont de Tours)
  7 (Amaury Vicomte de Thouars)
  Aimery IV Vicomte of Thouars, mentioned by
  William of Poitiers and Orderic, was
  undoubtedly at the Battle. He was son of
  Geoffrey, Vicomte of Thouars. He lived on into
  the reign of William Rufus. As a Poitevan family,
  Mr. Geoffrey White considered it of no interest to
  AngloNorman genealogy.
TIBOL
  5 (Tibol)
  8 (Honfroi de Tilleul)
  Cleveland III 400-402
  (=Tilliol)
TIBOUVILLA
  Loyd 102-103
TIBTOTE
  1 & 3 (Tibtote)
  Cleveland III 185-189
TIGERIVILLA
  Loyd 103
TILLEUL see TIBOL
TILLIERES
  4 (Baronz Tillieres)
  6 (Le sire de Tillieres)
TILLIOL see TIBOL
TILLY see TALLY
TINEL
  5 (Tinel)
  8 (Toustain Tinel)
  Turstinus Tinel 1086 ST
  Cleveland III 408
TINEUILLE
  1 (Tineuille)
  Cleveland III 204-205
TINGEZ
  5 (Tingez)
  Cleveland III 407-408
  (=Tingry)
  see also TENWIS
TINGRY see TINGEZ
TIPITOT
  5 (Tipitot)

TIRELL
1 & 3 (Tirell)
Cleveland III 197-200
TISON see TISOUN
TISOUN
5 (Tisoun)
7 & 8 (Gilbert Tison)
Gilbertus/Gislebertus
Tison/Tisun 1086 TC
TOARZ see THOUARS
TODENI see TOSNI
TOESNI see TOSNI
TOGET
1 & 3 (Toget)
Cleveland III 152
TOKE see TOUKE
TOLET
1 & 5 (Tolet)
Cleveland III 202-203
TOLIMER
5 (Tolimer)
Cleveland III 406
TOLLEMACH
1 (Tollemach)
Cleveland III 179-181
TOLOUS
1 (Tolous)
Cleveland III 182-183
TOMY see TOSNI
TONQUE
6 (Le sire de Tonque)
TONY see TOSNI
TORCHY
6 (Le Seneschall de Torchy;
Le sire de Torchy)
TOREL see TORELL
TORELL
1 (Torell)
3 (twice; Torel)
Cleveland III 205
TOREIGNY
Loyd 104
TORMEOR
4 (Tormeor)
TORNAI see THORNY
TORNAY see THORNY
TORNAL
Loyd 104
TORNEOR
4 (Del Torneor)
TORNIERES
4 (De Tornieres)
TORT
6 (Bertram le Tort)
TORTECHAPPELL
1 (Tortechappell)

Cleveland III 205
TORTEVAL
8 (Renaud de Torteval)
TOSE see TOWS
TOSNI
1 (Touny & Tomy)
5 (Tony)
6 (Le sire de Tony)
7 (Guillaume de Toeni; Robert
de Toeni; Raoul de Toeni,
Seig. d'Acquigny)
8 (Gerenger de Toeni; Guillaume de
Toeni; Ibert de Toeni; Juhel
de Toeni; Raoul de Toeni;
Robert de Toeni)
Ralph de Toeni 1086 ST
Berengerius/Radulfus/Robertus
de Todeni/Todeneio/
Toeni/Toenio 1086 TC
Cleveland III 171-177
(=Toesni)
Loyd 104 (Todeni)
Ralf de Tosni, Lord of Conches, mentioned by
William of Poitiers and Orderic, was
undoubtedly at the Battle. He was descended
from the brother of Hugh de Cavalcamp, the
Frenchman whom William Longsword made
Archbishop of Rouen; and is said to have been
descended (through some unknownmarriage)
from an alledged uncle of Rolf Ganger, named
Malahulc [or Hulc, as it is possible that instead of
"de stirpe Malahulcii" we should read "de stirpe
mala Hulcii"]. He inherited the office of banner-
bearer from Roger de Tosni, but is said to have
refused to carry the flag at the Battle of Hastings,
because he wished to take an active part in the
fray. The heiress of the English line married Guy
de Beauchamp, Earl of Warwick. From a cadet,
Robert de Stafford, a great landowner in 1086,
descended the Barons of Stafford, who ended in
the next century with an heiress Millicent,
ancestress of the historic house of Stafford, Earls
of Stafford and Dukes of Buckingham. From
Neel de Stafford (1086), who was possibly but not
certainly a member of the same family, descend
in the legitimate male line the Gresleys, who
retained their Domesday estate of Drakelow until
1931.
TOTELLES
1 (Totelles)
3 (Totels)
Cleveland III 206
TOTELS see TOTELLES
TOTENAIS
Judhel de Totenais 1086 TC
TOUAERS see THOUARS

TOUARS see THOUARS
TOUCHET see TUCHET
TOUKE
  1 (Touke)
  4 (Cil de Touke)
  5 (Tuk)
  Toka 1086 ST
  Cleveland III 183-185
  (=Toke/Tuke)
TOUNY see TOSNI
TOUQUES
  7 (Le Sire de Touques)
TOURBEVILLE see TURBERVILLE
TOURLAVILLE
  8 (Raoul de Tourlaville)
TOURNAY see THORNY
TOURNEBUT
  7 (Le Sire de Tournebut)
  8 (De Tournebut)
TOURNEUR
  6 (Le sire de Tourneur)
  7 (Le Sire de Tourneur)
TOURNEVILLE see TURNAVILLA
TOURS
  7 (Martin de Tours)
TOURYS
  5 (Tourys)
  Cleveland III 407
TOUSTAIN
  8 (Toustain)
TOWS
  3 (Tows)
  Cleveland III 343-344 (=Tose)
TRACIE see TRACY
TRACY
  1 & 2 & 5 (Tracy)
  4 (Cil de Tracie)
  6 (Le sire de Tracy)
  7 (Le Sire de Tracy)
  Cleveland III 155-157
  Loyd 104-106
TRAGOD
  2 (Tragod)
TRAIES
  1 (Traies)
  Cleveland III 177-179
  (=Thays=Tyas)
  see also THAYS
TRAILEI
  2 (Traylliz)
  5 (Treylly)
  8 (Geoffroi de Trelli)
  Goisfridus de Traillgi/
    Tralgi 1086 ST
  Cleveland III 404-405
  Loyd 106

TRAINELL
  1 (Trainell)
  3 (Traynel)
  Cleveland III 159
TRALGI see TRAILEI
TRANCHARD
  8 (Raoul Tranchard)
TRASSEL
  2 (Trassel)
TRAUERS
  1 (Trauers)
  Trauers 1086 ST
  Cleveland III 203-204
  see also TAUERS
TRAVILLE
  5 (Traville)
  Cleveland III 408
TRAYLEY see TRAILEI
TRAYNEL see TRAINELL
TREGOS see TREGOZ
TREGOZ
  4 (Cil de Tregoz)
  5 (Tregos)
  7 (Le Sire de Tregoz)
  Cleveland III 403-404
  Loyd 106
TRELLI see TRAILEI
TRENCHELION
  1 (Trenchelion)
  Cleveland III 193-194
TRENCHEUILE
  1 (Trencheuile)
  Cleveland III 192-193
TRESGOZ see TREGOZ
TREUERELL
  1 (Treuerell)
  Cleveland III 205
TREVILLE
  5 (Treville)
  Cleveland III 406-407
TREYLLY see TRAILEI
TRIBUS MINETIS
  Loyd 107
TRISON see TESSON
TRIUET see TRIVET
TRIVET
  1 (Triuet)
  5 (Trivet)
  Cleveland III 202
TROIS GROS
  6 (Le sire de Trois Gros)
TRONSEBOURS
  6 (Bonteuillam Tronsebours)
TROSSEBOT see TROUSBUT
TROUSBUT
  1 (Trousbut; Trusbote)

2 (Trussebot)
3 (Trusbut)
4 (Trossebot)
7 (Le Sire de Troussebot)
Cleveland III 157-159
TROUSSEBOT see TROUSBUT
TRUSBOTE see TROUSBUT
TRUSBUT see TROUSBUT
TRUSLOT
3 (Truslot)
TRUSSEBOT see TROUSBUT
TRUSSEL
1 (Trussel)
2 (Trussell)
3 & 5 (Trussell)
Cleveland III 159-161
TRUSSELL see TRUSSEL
TUCHET
1 & 3 & 5 (Tuchet)
7 (Le Sire de Touchet)
8 (De Touchet)
Cleveland III 152-155
TUIT
Loyd 107
TUK see TOUKE
TUKE see TOUKE
TURBEMER
2 (Turbemer)
TURBERVILLE
1 (Turburuile; Turbeuile)
2 (Turbevyle)
3 (Turbeuill)
5 (Tourbeville)
Cleveland III 189-191
TURBEUILE see TURBERVILLE
TURBEUILL see TURBERVILLE
TURBEVYLE see TURBERVILLE
TURBURUILE see TURBERVILLE
TURLAVILL see TURNAVILLA
TURLEY
5 (Turley)
Cleveland III 406
TURNAVILLA
7 (Le Sire de Tourneville)
8 (Raoul de Tourneville)
Radulfus de Turnauilla/
Turlauill' 1086 ST
TUROLD
7 (Turold)
Turold, shown in an early scene in France on the Bayeux Tapestry, the wording perhaps indicating a dwarf-like groom or perhaps a knight of Gui de Ponthieu. He may be identical with a tenant of the Bishop of Bayeux of that name listed in Domesday Book, but there is nothing to indicate that he was at the Battle.

TURUILE
1 & 3 (Turuile)
Cleveland III 191
Loyd 108 (Turville)
TURVILLE see TURUILE
TYAS see TRAIES
TYRIET
5 (Tyriet)
UMFRANVILLE
2 (Ounfravyle)
3 (Vmframuile)
5 (Umfraville)
7 (Robert d'Amfreville)
Cleveland III 349-352
Loyd 108
UMFRAVILLE see UMFRANVILLE
URINIE
4 (Cil d'Urinie)
7 (Le Sire d'Origny)
USHER see VSCHERE
VAACIE
4 (Sire de Vaacie)
VABERON see VALBADON
VADU
2 (Vadu)
VAL see LAVAL
VALBADUN see VALBADON
VALBADON
1 (Vaberon)
8 (Ansfroi de Vaubadon;
Osmond de Vaubadon;
Renouf de Vaubadon)
Ansfridus de Valbadon
1086 TC
Rannulfus de Valbadon
1086 ST
Cleveland III 250
Loyd 108 (Valbadun)
VAL DE SAIRE see ANDEUILE
VALEINES
Loyd 108
VALENCE
1 & 3 & 5 (Valence)
2 (Valens)
Cleveland III 224
VALENGER
1 (Valenger)
Cleveland III 228
VALENGES
1 (Valenges)
5 (Vallonis)
8 (Pierre de Valonges)
Petrus de Valonges/
Valongies/Valonis
1086 TC & ST
Cleveland III 257-258

84

see also VALIUE
VALENS see VALENCE
VALERIS see VALERS
VALERS
　1 (Valers)
　5 (Valeris)
　Cleveland III 238
De la VALET
　5 (De la Valet)
　Cleveland III 371-372
　(=Lanvallei)
VALINGFORD
　1 (Valingford)
　Cleveland III 250-251
　(=Wallingford)
VALIUE
　1 (Valiue)
　Cleveland III 251
　(=Valenges)
　see also VALENGES
VALLE BADONIS
　Osmundus de Valle badonis
　　1086 ST
VALLIBUS see VAU
VALLONIS see VALENGES
VALONGES see VALENGES
VALONIS see VALENGES
VANAY
　1 (Vanay) Cleveland III 242-244
　(=Vancy)
VANCORD see VANCORDE
VANCORDE
　1 (Vancorde)
　3 (Vancord)
VANCY see VANAY
VASDEROLL
　1 (Vasderoll)
　Cleveland III 250
VASSY see VEFFAY
VASSYE see VEFFAY
VATIERVILLE see WATERVILLE
VATORTE
　2 (Vatorte)
VATTEVILLE see WATERVILLE
VAUASOUR see VAVASOUR
VAUBADON see VALBADON
VAUS
　1 (Deuaus)
　2 & 5 (Vaus)
　3 (Devaus)
　7 (Robert de Vaux)
　8 (Aitard de Vaux;
　　Robert de Vaux)
　Robertus de Vals/Vallibus/
　　/Deuais/Deuals 1086 ST
　Aitardus de Vals 1086 ST

Cleveland I 294-299
　(=De Vaux)
VAUURUILE
　1 (Vauuruile)
　8 (Guillaume de Vauville)
　Cleveland III 239-240
　(=Vauville)
VAUVILLE see VAUURUILE
VAUX see VAUS
VAVASOR see VAVASOUR
VAVASOUR
　1 & 3 (Vauasour)
　5 (Vavasor)
　Cleveland III 225-227
VECI see VESCY
VEER see VERE
VEFFAY
　1 (Veffay)
　2 (Vessi)
　6 (Le sire de Vassye)
　7 (Ive de Vassy;
　　Robert de Vassy)
　Cleveland III 242 (=Vessay)
VEHIM see VEIM
VEIL see LEVEL
VEILLY
　Loyd 109
VEIM
　Loyd 109
VEIRNY　1 (Veirny)
　3 (Verny)
　Cleveland III 238-239
　(=Verney)
VENABLES
　1 & 5 (Venables)
　7 & 8 (Gilbert de Venables)
　Gislebertus de Venables
　　1086 ST
　Cleveland III 228-231
VENDER see VENDOUR
VENDORE see VENDOUR
VENDOUR
　1 (Vendore)
　3 (Vender)
　5 (Vendour)
　Cleveland III 227
VENEUR see VENOUR
VENICORDE
　1 (Venicorde)
　Cleveland III 251
　see also PENECORD
　　& FAUECOURT
VENIELS
　1 (Veniels)
VENOIS see VERNOYS
VENOUR

1 (Venoure)
5 (Venour)
7 (Raoul Le Veneur)
Cleveland III 231-236
(=Grosvenor)
VENOURE see VENOUR
VENUZ see VERNOYS
VER see VERE
VERBOIS see WARDEBOIS
VERDEIRE see VERDER
VERDENEL see WERDONELL
VERDER
1 (Verdeire)
3 (Verder)
5 (Verders)
Cleveland III 224-225
VERDERS see VERDER
VERDON see VERDUN
VERDOUN see VERDUN
VERDOUNE see VERDUN
VERDUN
1 (Verdoune)
2 (Verdoun)
3 (Verdon)
7 & 8 (Bertran de Verdun)
Bertrannus de Verdun 1086 TC
Cleveland III 221-224
Loyd 109
VERDYERS
2 (Verdyers)
VERE 1 (Delauere)
2 (Vere)
3 (de la Vere;
Aubrie de Vere)
5 (Veer)
8 (Guillaume de Ver)
Albericus/Willielmus de Ver
1086 ST
Cleveland I 331-332,
III 206-212
Loyd 110
VERLAND
1 & 3 (Verland)
5 (Veylaund)
Cleveland III 237-238
(=Wayland)
VERLAY
1 & 3 (Verlay)
Robertus de Verli/Verlei
1086 TC & ST
Hugo/Willielmus de Verlay
1086 ST
Cleveland III 227-228
Loyd 110 (Verleio)
VERLEIO see VERLAY
VERNEUIL see VRNALL

VERNEY see VEIRNY
VERNOIS see VERNOYS
VERNON
1 & 2 & 3 (Vernoun)
5 (twice; Vernoun)
7 & 8 (Gautier de Vernon;
Huard de Vernon;
Richard de Vernon)
Huardus de Vernun 1086 ST
Ricardus de Vernun/Vernon
1086 ST
Walterius de Vernon 1086 ST
Cleveland III 212-216
Loyd 110
VERNOUN see VERNON
VERNOYS
1 (Vernoys)
3 (Vernois)
7 & 8 (De Venois)
Cleveland III 244-248
(=Venois)
Loyd 109 (Venuz)
VERNUN see VERNON
VERNY see VEIRNY
VEROUN
5 (Veroun)
Cleveland III 413-414
VERRERE
1 (Verrere)
Cleveland III 241-242
VESCY
1 & 5 (Vescy)
8 (Ive de Veci; Robert de Veci)
Robertus de Veci 1086 TC
Cleveland III 216-220
VESLI
7 (Le Sire de Vesli)
8 (Hugue de Vesli;
Robert de Vesli)
VESSAY see VEFFAY
VESSI see VEFFAY
VEYLAUND see VERLAND
VEYN see VEIM
VEZ-PONT see VIPONT
VIAN
1 (Vian)
Cleveland III 244
VICOMTE
8 (Le Vicomte)
see also NEILE
VICTRY see VITRIE
VIELZ-PONT see VIPONT
VIEUXPONT see VIPONT
VIGOT see BIGOT
VILAIN see VILAN
VILAN

1 & 3 (Vilan)
5 (Vilain)
8 (Robert de Villon)
Cleveland III 236-237
VILERS
3 (Mesni-le-Villers)
7 (Godefroi de Villers)
Cleveland III 326-332
(=Villiers)
Loyd 111 (Vilers)
VILLERS see VILERS
VILLIERS see VILERS
VILLON see VILAN
VINOUN
2 & 5 (Vinoun)
Cleveland III 411-412
(=Vivonne)
VIPONT
2 (Vipoun),
4 (Dam Willame de Vez-Pont)
5 (Vipount)
6 (Guilliam de vielz Pont)
7 (Guillaume de Vieuxpont)
Cleveland III 409-411
VIPOUN see VIPONT
VIPOUNT see VIPONT
VIS DE LOUP see VISO LUPI
VISO LUPI
7 (Honfroi Vis de Loup)
8 (Honfroi Vis-de-Loup;
Raoul Vis-de-Loup)
Hunfridus Vis de Lew 1086 TC
Hunfridus Uisde Leuu/
Uisdelupo 1086 ST
Radulfus Viso lupi 1086 ST
VITAL
7 & 8 (Vital)
Vital, named on the Bayeux Tapestry in the
scenes between the landing and the Battle of
Hastings and therefore almost certainly at the
Battle. Two vassals, Vital and Wadard, are
supposed to be identical with tenants of the
Bishop of Bayeux so named in Domesday Book,
and were probably men of some local importance
at Bayeux.
VITOT
8 (Robert de Vitot)
When relating the doings of a certain Robert de
Vitot in 1063, Orderic adds that not long
afterwards, when the English War, in which he
was wounded in the knee, had been
accomplished, he contracted a mortal illness,
from which he died (apparently at Dover). It is
extremely likely that this relates to the
Expedition of 1066 and that he was wounded at
the Battle of Hastings, although it is not

impossible that the passage refers to later
fighting.

VITRIE
4 (Cil de Vitrie; twice)
6 (Le sire de Victry)
7 (Andre de Vitrie)
VIVILLE see VIUILLE
VIVONNE see VINOUN
VIUILLE
1 (Viuille)
8 (Hugue de Viville)
Cleveland III 251-257
(=Wydevile=Wyvill)
VMFRAMUILE see UMFRANVILLE
VNKET
1 & 3 (Vnket)
Cleveland III 249
VRNAFULL
1 (Vrnafull)
Cleveland III 249-250
VRNALL
1 & 3 (Vrnall)
Cleveland III 248-249
(=Verneuil)
VSCHERE
1 (Vschere)
Cleveland III 242 (=Usher)
VUASTENEYS
5 (Vuasteneys)
Cleveland III 412-413
(=Wasteneys)WACE
5 (Wace)
WACELAY
5 (Wacelay)
Cleveland III 414
WACELIN see WATELIN
WADARD
7 & 8 (Wadard)
Named on the Bayeux Tapestry in the scenes
between the landing and the Battle of Hastings
and therefore almost certainly at the Battle. Two
vassals, Wadard and Vital, are supposed to be
identical with tenants of the Bishop of Bayeux so
named in Domesday Book, and were probably
men of some local importance at Bayeux.
WAFRE
1 (Wafre)
Cleveland III 258-259
WAKE
1 & 2 & 3 (Wake)
5 (De Wake)
Cleveland III 259-262
WAKEVYLE
2 (Wakevyle)
WALANGAY

87

5 (Walangay)
Cleveland III 414
WALEDGER
3 (Waledger)
Cleveland III 352
(=Warenger)
WALEYS see WALOYS
WALLINGFORD see VALINGFORD
WALOYS
5 (Waloys)
Cleveland III 415
(=Waleys= Walsh)
WALSH see WALOYS
WALTERVILLA
Loyd 111
WALUILE
Willielmus de Waluile 1086 ST
WAMERVILE
5 (Wamervile)
Cleveland III 414
WANCEIO see WANCY
WANCEIS see WANCY
WANCI see WANCY
WANCY
5 (Wauncy)
7 (Hugue de Wanci;
Osberne de Wanci)
8 (Osberne de Wanci)
Hugo/Osbernus de Wanceio
1086 ST
Loyd 111
WANZ
Aluric Wanz 1086 TC
De la WAR see DELAWARE
WARBEVYLE
2 (Warbevyle)
WARD see DELAWARD
WARDE see DELAWARD
WARDEBOIS
1 (Wardebois)
2 (Wardeboys)
3 (Wardebus)
5 (Verbois)
Cleveland III 258
WARDEBUS see WARDEBOIS
WAREINE see WARENNE
WAREN see WARENNE
WARENGER see WALEDGER
WARENNE
1 (Wareine)
2 (Warenne)
3 (Waren)
4 (Willeme de Garenes)
5 (Warenne)
6 (Guilliam de Garennes)
7 (Guillaume de Warren)

8 (Guillaume de Warenne)
Willelmus de Warenna/Warene
1086 TC
Cleveland III 262-266
Loyd 111-112
William de Warenne, afterwards 1st Earl of
Surrey, mentioned by William of Poitiers and
Orderic, was undoubtedly at the Battle. He was
the younger son of a certain Rodulf de Warenne,
and had already gained the favour of the Duke
by his gallantry at the Battle of Mortemer. His
grandson William, 3rd Earl of Surrey, left an
heiress from whom descended the later family of
Warenne, Earls of Surrey.
WARLEY
5 (Warley)
WARROYS
5 (Warroys)
Cleveland III 414
WASPAIL see WESPAILE
WASPREY
Loyd 112
WASPRIA
Loyd 112
WAST
Nigellus Wast 1086 ST
Loyd 112
WASTENEYS see VUASTENEYS
de la WATCH see DELUACHE
WATE
1 (Wate)
3 (Wate & de la Wate)
Cleveland III 266-269
WATELIN
1 (Watelin)
3 (Wateline)
Cleveland III 269-270
(=Wacelin)
WATELINE see WATELIN
WATERVILE see WATERVILLE
WATERVILLE
1 (Wateuil)
2 (Watervyle)
3 (Wateuile)
5 (Watervile; Waterville)
8 (Guillaume de Vatteville;
Richard de Vatteville;
Robert de Vatteville)
Robertus de Wateuile 1086 TC
Ricardus/Robertus/Willielmus
de Wateuile 1086 ST
Cleveland III 270-272
Loyd 111
WATEVILE see WATERVILLE
WATEVILLE see WATERVILLE
WAUNCY see WANCY

WAVILLE
  5 (twice; Waville)
WAYLAND see VERLAND
WELY
  1 (Wely)
  Cleveland III 272
WEMERLAY
  5 (Wemerlay)
  Cleveland III 414
WERDONELL
  1 (Werdonell)
  Cleveland III 272 (=Verdenel)
WERDOUN
  5 (Werdoun)
WERLAY
  5 (Werlay)
WESPAILE
  1 (Wespaile)
  Cleveland III 273 (=Waspail)
WIDUILE
  Hugo de Widuile 1086 TC
WIRCE
  Goisfridus de Wirce 1086 ST
WISCAND/WISCANT
  8 (Gilbert de Wissant)
  Gislebertus de Wiscand/
    Wiscant/Wissand/Witsand
    /Witsthant 1086 ST
WISSAND see WISCAND
WISSANT see WISCAND
WITSAND see WISCAND
WITSTHANT see WISCAND
WITVILE see WYVILE
WIUELL see WYVILE
WOLY
  3 (Woly)
WYDEVILE see VIUILLE
WYUELL see WYVILE
WYVILE
  1 (Wiuell)
  3 (Wyuell)
  5 (Wyvile)
  Hugo de Wituile 1086 ST
WYVILL see VIUILLE
YLE see ISLE
YLEBON
  2 (Ylebon)
ZOUCHE see SOUCH

89